PINSTRIPE PLANET

Fine Lines from the World's Best

PINSTRIPE PLANET

Fine Lines From the World's Best

General Editor
HERB MARTINEZ

KORERO

This edition published in 2006 by Korero Books LLP,
32 Great Sutton Street, Clerkenwell, London, EC1V 0NB, UK

ISBN-13: 978-0-9553-3980-6
ISBN-10: 0-9553-3980-6

A Korero Books LLP production.

CONTENTS

1 SHOT

IN THE BEGINNING

Drawing the line is embedded deep in man's pysche. You could argue that it all started with those 23,000 year-old cave paintings discovered, perfectly preserved, in Southern France and Spain. Later, the Romans, Celts, and Anglo-Saxons, amongst others, were into it for decorating their chariots.

By the 18th Century line art was decorating most smart carriages: a line, a single stroke of paint, was used to accentuate the shape and grace of the vehicle. Canal boats looked pretty good with simple striping too. Even Henry Ford, that master of simplicity and exponent of the color black, couldn't resist: countless model A's were adorned with striping paint right at the factory. In time, however, fashions changed, and the last American car manufacturer producing automobiles with striping was General Motors, in 1938.

A number of trends converged to revive striping as an expression of the counter culture. The beginnings of hot-rodding in Southern California resulted in hugely imaginative decoration designed to transform second-hand Fords (which were cheap and relatively easy to hop-up for extra power) into unique racing machines. As racing on city streets became dangerous and illegal, enthusiasts turned to the dry lakes east of Los Angeles, which became weekend testing grounds for speed.

World War II rudely interrupted the fun, but it provided the young men of California with the opportunity to spread the Hot Rod word and would lay the foundations for the "golden age" of pinstriping in the '50s and '60s. After the war, big companies such as Bell Laboratories and Lockheed set up offices in California. Many of their employees were ex-servicemen with a cavalier attitude as well as a technical bent. The adrenaline rush of the battlefield was being replaced with the thrill of speed trials. Just as some of the men had painted their combat aircraft with nose art and flames during the war, so they started doing the same to their hopped-up cars.

Pinstriping, scallops and flames may have predated World War II as stylistic devices, but it was in the postwar period that they really made their mark. Just as hot rod culture evolved as an antidote to the cultural conformity of the 1950s, pinstriping became one of the cornerstones of Kustom Kulture, the visual expression of the Californian hot rod culture scene. The spirit of alienation and rebellion, which is part of the pinstriping tradition, is a direct result of these wartime experiences and a reaction to 1950s establishment culture.

The scene was pioneered by relatively few individuals who found that they had a passion and talent for painting The Line. We feature these men in our Pioneers section. Von Dutch was perhaps the most influential, and true to the spirit of modern pinstriping's origins, he had no appetite for the media circus which later developed around him.

That California generation spawned what is now a global phenomenon. In these pages we provide a survey of some of the major artists currently carrying this energy-charged artform forward in the East, Midwest, and West-Coast of the USA, as well as in Japan, Australia, and Europe.

Each of our artists gives some insight into their work, how they got started, and their sources of inspiration. More than anything, however, we want you to view the fantastic imagery they have created, and hope that this pure form of art, unencumbered by any art-world curated process, will in turn inspire.

PIONEERS OF MODERN STRIPING

Right: Von Dutch in his Reseda, California garage,1966. Donovan's future wife Linda Lawrence's back is freshly pinstriped. © 2006 Photo by Barry Feinstein.

Kenneth Howard, a.k.a. Von DUTCH

In 1996 the rights to the name Von Dutch were sold to entrepreneur Michael Cassel. Within five years there were Von Dutch stores across the globe: in Tokyo, Moscow, London, Milan, Mexico City, Paris, Rome, Bangkok as well as in Miami, Chicago, Santa Monica and New Jersey. A fabulous logo spoke of the cool range of clothing and accessories: a bit of Kustom Kulture for the High Street, but a far cry from the origins and lifestyle behind the name.

Few of the customers of these stores would know in any detail who or what Von Dutch was. In a nutshell he was Kenneth Francis Howard, and what he was was the father of modern decorative pinstriping. Beatnik artist, machinist extraordinare and cult hero, Von Dutch would be astonished were he aware of how his name today straddles the globe, fronting retail outlets.

Von Dutch was simply not interested in money, disliked celebrity, and avoided publicity. He once said that he made a point of staying on the poverty line. He didn't exploit his own name because he didn't want to. Paradoxically, it is precisely because he was such an anti-confirmist original, that the brand Von Dutch has the resonance it has today. Howard, born in 1929, grew up in South Central Los Angeles near Watts, in the Huntington Park and then Compton neighborhoods. His father was a sign painter who specialized in gold leaf on doors, and whose commissions included City Hall and UCLA. In his teenage years, Kenny never was much of a schoolboy. They say he jumped out of a second floor schoolroom window one day, into a tree, and never came down, so to speak.

The L.A. of the 1950s was a flourishing centre of beat culture, and Von Dutch quickly picked up on the vibe around motorcycles and motorcycle shops. He also found that striping bikes could, to his surprise, get him enough funds to survive. He started striping cars as a joke. The joke quickly – in 1951 – turned into a flourishing business, and his illustrious career of pinstriping, auto painting, and lettering took off. Everyone by the mid 1950s wanted their car or motorcycle "Dutched".

But Von Dutch couldn't settle down. He moved from South Central up to Hollywood, then to the San Fernando valley, out to Arizona, and then back to California. He was obsessed for a while about a move to Australia, so he could plug into Surf culture, but this he never realized.

His creative journey, however, was massive. From pinstriping for cars, he expanded into canvases, signs, and even T-shirts and sweatshirts, becoming, in effect, the first exponent of airbrushing on T-shirts. When he tired of painting, he went full time into machining and mechanics, creating cars and bikes for Hollywood movies including *The Reivers* and *Le Mans*. Through his movie work he acquired private commissions from a number of stars, and also built a car for Steve McQueen.

Given to bouts of psychological upheaval, Dutch's mood swings could result in periods when he would ignore friends, customers, and the world in general. He was not interested in commercial success, and as long as he could feed his alcohol and smoking habit, he seemed happy (in the end it was probably the two that killed him, aged only 62). In 1958 he decided to turn his back on his increasing commercial success and celebrity status in L.A., adopted a gypsy lifestyle out of a converted Long Beach city bus and then, in 1970, moved to Arizona. The Arizona years saw Dutch continue his work, and some of his most innovative designs come from this period.

We don't know the precise reasons, but after five years in the desert, Dutch was back in California, where he took up a residency at Movieworld Cars of the Stars in Buena Park, CA – one of the centres of Kustom Kulture – painting, motorizing and creating many of the exhibits. When the attraction closed in the early 1980s, he moved with the collection to the Brucker Brothers ranch in Santa Paula, near Oxnard, CA, and stayed there until his death in 1992.

Von Dutch was an original, but it wasn't just his innovations which earned him the status of Father of Modern Pinstriping. It was also his innate talent for the art. His ability to create a mirror image of his designs, working from side to side, has never been

Above: Detail of Von Dutch's paintbox (originally his dad's, Walker Howard). Photo by Al Quattrocchi; collection of Jim and Danny Brucker.

The iconic bloodshot flying eyeball was first used by Von Dutch. He got the idea from 5000-year old Macedonian and Egyptian imagery (which represented an all-seeing flying eyeball in outline form) and added the bloodshot detail. The design has mutated over the years: you find it everywhere now, to the point where it's almost a counter-culture cliché seen on T-shirts, skateboards, record covers and stickers.

Von Dutch working on what was described at the time as "the unbroken line" on the hood of George Barris's '49 Ford shop wagon. The wagon appeared in color on the cover of the March 1955 issue of *Rod & Custom*. Dutch apparently did this job while locked in Barris's shop one night.

bettered. He also had the knack of getting an artwork measurably and perfectly centered in the middle of a panel. He could stripe one side of a car and then the other, executing the same design in the same places, without needing to refer back to the original. In his heyday he was truly considered The Master, although he, with typical modesty, felt that Tommy the Greek in Oakland, CA, had it all over him. To Dutch it was all about the quality. The visual eye was his master, and he captured that point with his creation of the "flying eyeball" in the 1950s.

More than anything, Von Dutch liked to be considered a master machinist and fabricator. He never used the word 'artist' to describe what he did. He once said that he would have liked to have been just a gunsmith (guns and knives had become another Von Dutch fascination). For someone of such cultural significance, it is curious that not until 2002, a decade after his death, was Von Dutch featured in a solo exhibition. The show, held at the California State University Northridge art facility, was entitled *Von Dutch: An American Original.* That's one title, when attached to Kenneth Francis Howard, that is beyond argument.

Top: Detail of Dutch's hand engraving on a Winchester .22-caliber rifle. Photo by Al Quattrocchi.
Middle: Grille of John Goad's Duece three window coupe, striped by Von Dutch in 1971. Photo by Aaron Kahan; collection of John Goad.
Bottom: Detail of Stan Betz's El Camino, painted and pinstriped by Von Dutch in 1982. Photo by Al Quattrocchi.

Ed Roth

Ed "Big Daddy" Roth was born in Beverly Hills in 1932. His family were typical German immigrants coping with the depression. Ed's father, a cabinet maker by trade, made his living as a personal driver for a wealthy Beverly Hills widow, Mrs Gott. Ed inherited his father's practical side and ability to make things. He also took art classes in high school. He left in 1951, and did 4 years in the U.S. Air Force, where Ed earned extra money by lettering servicemen's duffel bags. Ed returned to Southern California and took up pinstriping in his driveway. "Ed learned pinstriping on his own – he just picked it up," according to his brother Gordon.

The area in Maywood where Ed settled was a hotbed of hot rod and custom creativity. Pinstriping was still quite rare, with just Von Dutch, Larry Watson and Dean Jeffries specializing. In 1956, Ed became a pinstriper too, offering to stripe and flame a complete car for $4, when Von Dutch was charging $10. Ed at this point worked at Sears as a window dresser, leaving at 4pm to go and stripe in his newly opened shop on Firestone in Southgate. In 1957, Roth went into business with Bud "The Baron" Crozier and Tom Kelly. They called their outfit "The Crazy Painters," and opened a shop on Atlantic Boulevard. They had a reputation for scallops, flames, and striping, and also developed what Kelly called the "weirdo shirt" sideline. By 1959 Ed had outgrown The Crazy Painters, and he opened his own shop at 4616 Slauson in Maywood, undercutting The Crazy Painters's prices. He then switched direction, buying old cars and customizing them. Ever restless, he soon tried something new: building cars from scratch using junkyard parts, plaster, and fiberglass. Ed went on to create some of the most memorable custom cars ever built, beginning with the revolutionary "Outlaw" and following with the "Beatnik Bandit" in 1961. Both were immortalized by Revell in the '60s as model kits. Revell, or more specifically their VP of PR Henry Blankfort, also gave him his "Big Daddy" moniker, a reference to his 6'3" height and 275 pounds weight.

At this point Ed was making more money than he knew what to do with, much of it from royalties from the Revell model kits (over 3 million were sold in 1964). The anti-hero *Rat Fink*, a character created by Roth

Left: An early photo of Ed Roth, courtesy of George Barris.

Below: A classic Ed Roth pose with his signature hat, in Vegas, 1995.

Left: Von Dutch's can of 1 Shot sitting on the roof of Ed Roth's Honda car. Striping by Roth. Photo by Al Quattrocchi; collection of Jim and Danny Brucker.

Below: Ed commissioned many artists – this is one example: a Paul Barrow T-shirt design ("Junkyard Brother") of *Rat Fink*.

on either a napkin or his refrigerator door, became an even bigger success. The paradox was that Ed started life as a recognized, and highly-skilled, striper, who first made it big by creating cars from scratch. Everyone knew he wasn't that good at inking and yet *Fink*, an inked line art figure, became his greatest commercial success.

Where Roth was particularly talented, and why his influence has been so huge, was in spotting new trends, much of the time by connecting with teen culture. In the '50s he knew it was hot rodding; in the '60s he got into surf culture early; he spotted the trend for the Maltese, or iron, cross early; when Honda 50 bikes became hot in 1965, Ed was already there; by 1966 he was leading the new fashion for choppers and trikes, with huge success.

Then Roth entered his "hiatus" phase, when his divorce in 1970 resulted in Roth Studio closing down. Ed went to work for Jim Brucker's Cars of the Stars museum in Buena Park, and then, in 1975, to the Knott's Berry Farm art department. Even during his quiet phase Ed couldn't help creating another great legacy: the Rat Fink Reunions, which were first held at Cars of the Stars in 1977, as a sort of re-creation of the

Roth employee Christmas parties of the 1960s. These became a major nexus for the exchange of ideas on pinstriping, and brought in a whole new generation of stripers. Roth became a Mormon and moved to Utah, where the Rat Fink Reunions continued, and began to build cars again. The painting and striping of *Rat Fink* trash cans for children's charities became a particular tradition.

Roth died suddenly in 2001. His was a big and complex life. Almost every striper in these pages claims him as a major influence, but it is his massive cultural impact, rather than his pinstriping in particular, which is being recognized here. His biographer Pat Ganahl refers to Ed's unique mix of "vivacity, capriciousness, creativity and compassion;" add massive natural talent to the mix and that might begin to do him justice.

Right: Pool cue ball shift knob painted by Ed Roth. Photo by Aaron Kahan; collection of Verne Hammond.
Below: Ed Roth striping a glove box in the early '60s.

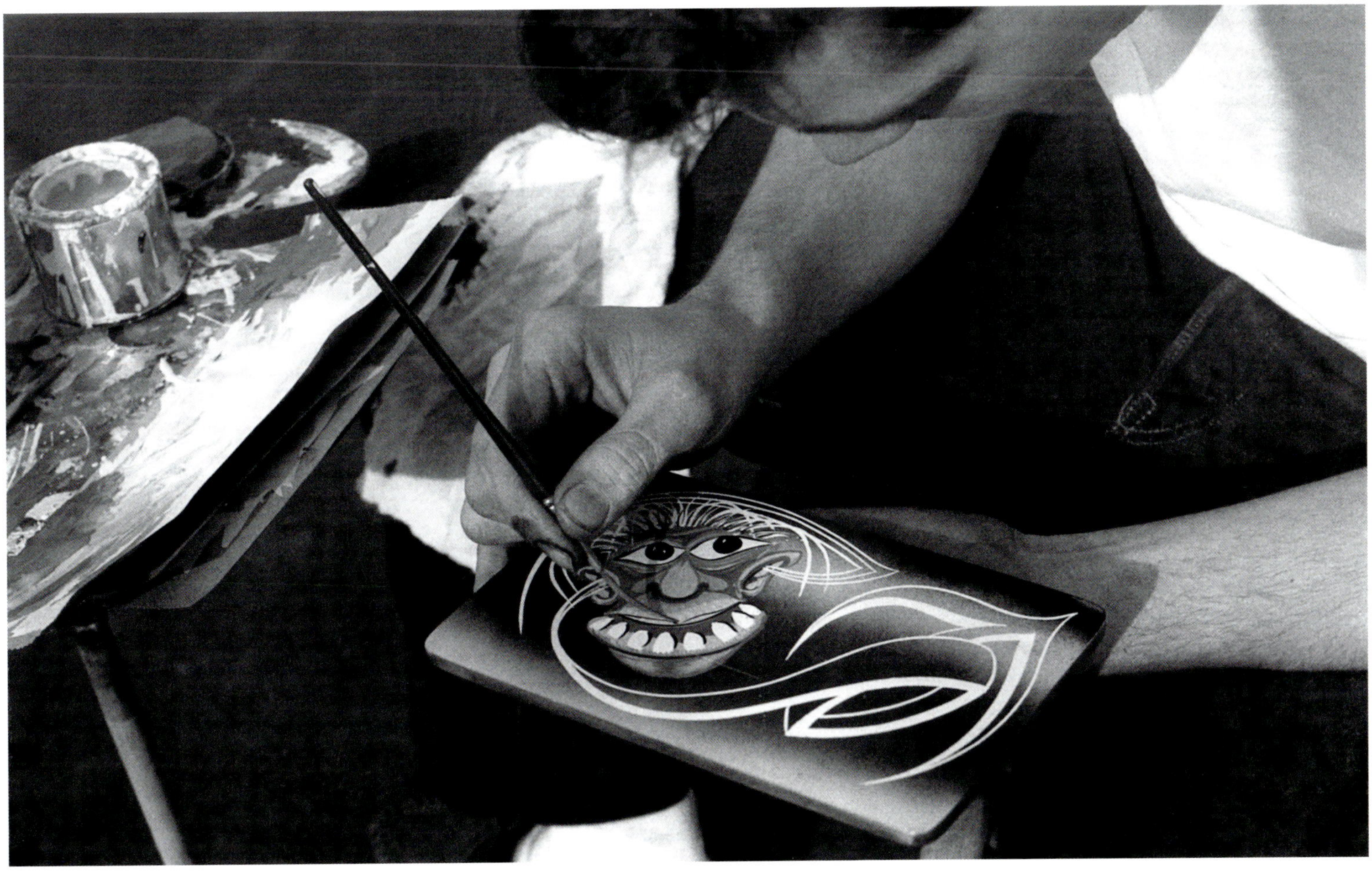

Tommy the Greek

In 2002 Tommy "The Greek" Hrones died aged 88. It was truly the passing of a legend, whom Von Dutch numbered as one of his primary influences. By many on the scene he was considered the best striper bar none, and also the most influential – to quote one afficionado's view, "You see many more cars in California today bearing the stamp of Tommy than you see wearing the Von Dutch look."

The eldest of eight children born to Greek immigrants who settled in Emeryville, Oakland, CA, Tommy had one of the classic routes into striping, being apprenticed in his uncle's Oakland paint shop. It was tough jack-of-all-trades laboring work. However, Uncle John had a shaky hand, and Tommy was given the job of striping the lines. This was what he discovered he was good at.

These were the days when most cars in the USA were produced with stripes of one kind or another, when Ford stripers earnt a premium over other assembly line workers. It wasn't yet a counter-cultural art form. Tommy, however, began to experiment and in so doing began to develop a truly individual style. The catalyst was meeting a freehand striper called Neils Hoegsberg, a recent Danish immigrant who did the rounds of the paintshops. By 1929 Tommy had already created his signature teardrops (perhaps his most influential design motif), scallops, arrows, and hashmarks.

Tommy started experimenting with customs in the mid-30s, restyling a '36 Ford Phaeton in the Cadillac La Salle mould. An endless stream of projects followed as Tommy's work got better known: fire engines, airplanes, Jim Hurtubise's Indy car, and the Stanley Dollar hydroplane "Hawaii Kai," in addition to a stack of motorbikes, dragsters and helmets. "Even toilet seats," according to Tommy.

With the talent went the often mercurial personality. Tyler Hoare, of West Coast Kustom Cruisin', puts it best: "The 15 minutes of fame is the easy part. The rest is the hard part. Tommy has always known who he is and what he's doing. He's a Picasso... with the same personality as Picasso."

Like Picasso, the stories of Tommy are legion. Art Himsl recalls being at a show in Oakland in the late '50s, doing a striping demo and having a tough time laying a straight line: "There was a crowd and from the back a voice, "Hey kid, hav'n a hard time? Can't hold that line?' After 10 minutes I'd had enough, and handed the brush to the agitator. It was Tommy. Zip. Zip. The job was done. He said, "Here's my card, kid."

It was this approach that earned Tommy his legendary status. As Himsl declared, "If you wanted your car done right, you took it to the Greek."

Tommy hugely influenced everyone around him. Herb Martinez, buzzing around his Oakland neighborhood on his bike as a boy, discovered Tommy's workshop, "always stacked with neat cars outside. If it hadn't been for Tommy allowing me to hang around his shop, I'd never have continued striping the way I have. Heck, I'm still doing teardrops after 38 years."

Martinez remembers the impact of seeing him in full flood: "He was an absolute master, and fast. There was a "wham-bam" ritual about his work. He'd open a can of Veco lacquer with an ice pick, step back, fire the ice pick into the wall... Ping!... Set up like a rocket, stripe the car, bait and antagonize the customers, and finish up the job."

Cary Greenwood, a Northern Californian striper, also remembers seeing Tommy at work. He in turn opened his own shop and Tommy would send him work: "real klunkers!" However his admiration is undiminished: "He's been overlooked because of the Von Dutch mystique. Nobody ever striped straighter than Tommy the Greek."

Tommy's was an intense life, lived fast. He owned over 75 cars in his time, mostly Caddy sedans, and a load of Harleys, Triumphs and Indian motorbikes. He closed his last working shop in 1994, aged 80, but kept tinkering with small restoration and painting projects. He also found time to feed many of Oakland's stray animals, and for the occasional round of golf.

Tommy once said, "If your car wasn't done by me you weren't nothing." Art Himsl put it another way: "God himself went to The Greek."

Left: Tommy doing an inpromptu striping demo. The picture dates from the late '40s.

Below: Tommy the Greek in U.S. Navy uniform with his landmark street custom '40 Merc convertible which he owned from 1943 to 1947.

Dean Jeffries

Dean Jeffries is one of the last of the legendary stripers, from the early Southen California pinstriping craze, who can still tell what the scene back in the early 1950s was really like. His obsession with the art remains: every day he goes to his workshop even though he is now retired and the shop has been closed to the public for many years.

Dean was born in Lynwood, California in 1933. He grew up within a quarter mile of the famous Barris Kustom City in Lynwood, no doubt an early influencing factor on his later life choices. On graduating high school in 1949 Dean promptly enlisted in the Army where he was stationed in Germany, as a map maker: the guy could clearly draw. On completing his tour of duty he decided not to follow his dad's footsteps as an auto mechanic. Instead, he picked up a brush and started doing pinstriping and custom paint.

Von Dutch was an early influence and helped Dean early on, even showing him where to get his paint and brush supplies. Dean's signature became the speed at which he could work. Where Dutch would take a whole day to do a car, Dean would get it done by lunch time.

Dean got a job at George Cerni's shop and his unlikely first striping commission was a boat. His first car, a 1947 Merc, exhibited all his precocious expertise in flaming, striping, and drawing. Dean recalls that in those days, you got $25 for flaming and striping a

Left: Dean Jeffries putting some stripes on a helmet.

Opposite Page: Striping the decklid (trunk lid) of his '47 Mercury convertible.

whole car. Setting up independently, Dean rented a shop next to Barris's on Atlantic Blvd. In addition to his private commissions, George Cerni passed over all his striping work to Dean. Some of the cars he worked on on Atlantic Blvd were legendary customs like Johnny Zupan's Merc, Bill Carr's "Aztec," and the famous "Ala Kart" that won America's Most Beautiful Roadster back in 1958-59. He flamed and pinstriped the "Kookie Car" T-roadster used on TV's 77 Sunset Strip and, perhaps most famously, he lettered "Little Bastard" on the back of the 1956 Porsche in which James Dean crashed and was immortalized.

Dean opened his second shop on Sunset Blvd. Also on Sunset was Kustom Kulture publishers Petersen Publications and, unsurprisingly, Dean became their lead writer on How-To techniques, enthusing and influencing a broad audience. Established and successful by 1959, Dean was a fixture on the scene, driving a customized 356 Porsche coupe and spending many weekends at local racing tracks. His circle of friends in the Indy scene included J.C. Agaganian, Parnelli Jones, and A. J. Foyt, and through these contacts more commissions flowed in. In 1959 alone he painted nearly a dozen Indy 500 cars, some featuring modern flames for the first time.

Getting busier meant another move, this time to Hollywood, to the shop that he still occupies today. Dean diversified and started working metal, creating his famous "Manta Ray." Created for the Oakland Roadster Show and inspired by Bill Cushenbery's famous "Silhouette," Dean entered the car in the prestigious Tournament of Fame and won. He got a trip to the Paris Auto Show with his car. While in Europe he managed a few side trips to the race track in France and Italy.

Once back home he was asked by AMT to use his car as a model for one of their kits. He also made inroads into the Hollywood studio scene when the car was used in a few movies. Dean began to make cars to commission from the studios. He built such famous cars as the "Green Hornet", the "Monkee

Above: Jeffries in his studio in the late '50s (note the coif), airbrushing a shirt, similar to the one he is wearing.
Below: Dean Jeffries striping hub caps for *Rod and Custom* magazine.
Below Left: Dean striping the outlines on flames.

Opposite Page: Dean Jeffries striping a spider's web around the antenna (aerial) of his '47 Mercury convertible.

Mobile," the fiberglass body for the "Kyote," and the Landmaster from the movie *Damnation Alley*. His personal car was a radically chopped, channeled, and sectioned '34 Ford sedan with major-sized red, orange, and yellow flames. He still owns the '34 and the Manta Ray, and they have been displayed at the Petersen Museum in nearby Los Angeles. Not bad for a guy who started pinstriping cars in Lynwood.

Above: Norm Grabowski's Chevrolet Corvair flat-6 powered bike as striped by Dean Jeffries.

Opposite Page: Dean Jeffries striping a dash at the Barris Shop.

Tom Kelly

The early '50s were the heyday of modern pinstriping, and it was all happening around the L.A. basin. Tom Kelly was one of the legendary small group, which included Von Dutch, Tommy the Greek, Ed Roth and "The Baron", who made the scene take off. Today, Tom is the last one still striping.

Born in Temple City, a suburb of L.A., in 1940, Tom was hooked on drawing from an early age. At age 13 he started working with his grandfather, none other than the legendary D.Z. Crozier, a.k.a "The Baron," who used Tom's precocious skills on dashboards whilst he striped the rest of the car. It was a heady and busy time: Von Dutch was changing all notions of what auto decoration meant, and The Baron's team of artists were fantastically busy, sometimes working on 8-10 cars a day.

It was the best possible apprenticeship. One day Tom was messing around with some striping on a customer's pickup tailgate. The Baron came round the back, saw the design, and said "Leave it on." "It was then that I really started striping," says Tom, who as a result was raised to $10 a week.

The Baron and Tom used to regularly check out other stripers. Hearing of a new shop which had opened in Southgate, they wandered around to see some pretty impressive work. The owner of the shop was Ed "Big Daddy" Roth, and the instant chemistry between the three resulted a few weeks later in the formation of The Crazy Painters – Ed, The Baron and Kelly. They worked together until 1959, when Ed started his own studio in Maywood.

Tom and The Baron carried on the business until 1962, when the Baron died. His instruction to Tom was: "I don't want you at my funeral, I want to know that you'll be working that day." Tom carried out that instruction to the letter. At the time, Mitch, Tom's son, was just three years old. But as the years went by Mitch got involved in the workshop, sanding and tapping cars for painting, and learning all aspects of the business, just as Tom had with The Baron.

Today Tom and Mitch still work together and the business is now called Kelly and Son, The Crazy Painters. It is amazing to think that this is a paintshop now in its third generation but still with the same core ethos of the early '50s.

Tom is enthused by the way striping has become a worldwide phenomenon and the way the art is always mutating and developing. He loves to encourage new talent: "The possibilities with striping are endless. There's always room for another striper, so come on in, the water's fine!"

Above Left: Tom Kelly in his studio, 2005.
Left: The young Tom Kelly at a show in the '50s, demonstrating airbrush work on sweatshirts.

Lyle Fisk

Like Tom Kelly, Lyle Fisk was born in 1940, and like Tom also, he is still hard at work striping and creating great new work.

His family lived in Coalinga, CA, renowned as an earthquake spot. At the age of 10 he became car crazy. Drawing cars was what he did, rather than his regular schoolwork. In his spare time he worked at a sign shop in Coalinga and striped his first car, aged 15, in 1955: "It was a '48 Chevy coupe. I drove it down to Main Street. The rest is history."

Soon renowned for his striping talents, Lyle's commissions started coming through quickly. He was recognized for his overall design ability, but in particular for his gold-leaf work and antique striping. Lyle is also credited for inventing the "feather" design which is now a staple of pinstripe decoration: the technique is particularly useful, as it allows a long area to be filled with filigree.

While he has flown to paint commissions all over the US, Lyle has stayed rooted in California, moving his studio first to San Diego and then to Ramona, a small farming town 20 miles to the northeast.

Typically modest, Lyle credits all his influences: "There were some great people who worked with me – Ron Muller and John Wysocki were the best – and it was fantastic to be working around fellows like Von Dutch, Ed Roth and Chuck "Shakey Jake" Babbit. They were huge – real icons of the industry."

And what of pinstriping itself? Lyle reflects on what an amazing world it is and how, in a 50-year career, he has had more fun "than should be allowed." He also reflects on its unpredictability – "Just when you think it's about to die off, the work goes through the roof !"

His one regret (and ours too) is that so much of his work has gone unrecorded. "In the early days photography was expensive and we didn't have the money or the attitude to record our work." The more recent work is much better documented and will continue to be so – Lyle has no plans to retire yet.

Below: Lyle Fisk in 1972 showing his paintwork on the Silver and Gold Racing Team van.

Craig Judd

A son of Chowchilla, in the San Joaquin Valley, CA, Craig Judd discovered his natural ability for art at high school, but his conversion to the scene he can date specifically: "It was in 1966 in a Fresno CA car lot, and the car was a lowered '61 Cadillac with a beautiful stripe job; it was by Neil Averil. I knew then I wanted to be a striper!"

The Fresno scene was hot in those days – "I had to get good or get out," Craig recalls. On the main drag in Fresno (Blackstone Avenue), "75% of the cars and trucks were striped – like a free car show every day." After a short stint in a local body shop and some time at a GM training school, Judd opened his own shop in 1974, and by 1976 was doing only custom work.

Judd sees himself very much as part of a specific Fresno scene, which grew organically from the talents which congregated and collaborated there. "I don't think back then that those artists knew they were contributing to the scene, or how huge it would become, but the best stripers were in Fresno."

He points to some significant characters who had a big influence on him: Neil Averill, Bob Kovac and Dale "Stodgy" Oftedal. "Neil was the King of Cool. He developed so many new techniques. He was the first to put a thin line down the middle of a 1/4 inch band stripe, and the first to put a scroll on the end of a double line: he is probably the most influential exponent of a 'Fresno Style'." Bob Kovac he celebrates for his color combinations, and Dale, who worked with Bob, for his ability to load a brush with two colors and blend one color into another in a thin line.

Judd is characteristically modest about his own achievements. The fact remains that he is hugely influential in his own right and one of the best stripers working in the US. He has striped numerous iconic machines, including the famous 1950 Studebaker "Panic Parrot" for Steve Metz's Hotrod Underground.

Judd is also consciously inspiring a younger crowd to take up striping (he calls it "The Art Form" and is pleased that it is now being recognized as such). He holds regular pinstriping workshops with hands-on training and has produced two instructional videos: *Pinstriping Made Easy* and *Flames Made Easy*. He is happy for others to copy his work – "Hey, it's the greatest form of flattery." Two "new kids on the block" stripers he mentions are Greg "The Kid" Gonzalez and Jimmy Ogawa.

More than forty years after he started, Craig is still striping. He works with his wife, Sally, and they have been in the same studio in Chowchilla, 35 miles from Fresno, since 1977; "She is my best critic and puts up with my 'artistic' mood swings." He loves what he does: "It wasn't easy to get to this point in the striping game, but then no one ever said it would be. If I had to live my life again would I take the same route ? You bet I would."

Left: Craig Judd today, laying down the line on a fender.

Dave Bell

In 1956 Dave Bell, then at high school, picked up a copy of *Car Craft* magazine and saw an article on Von Dutch: "I couldn't believe my eyes – here was a guy who was combining hot rod rebellion with Salvador Dali-like abstractions. I was hooked."

He knew when he graduated high school in 1957 that he would make his living as an artist, although exactly how did not become clear until his family travelled around Southern California: "There were cool cars everywhere. I went to Lynwood and saw Barris's shop and on the way out saw a Dean Jeffries '46 Merc. That evening, down a side street and with a great crowd gathered around it, there was Norm Grabowski's "Kookie Car" T roadster. When I got home I knew I had to get into this striping thing, so I tried it out, and on some sweatshirts too."

Dave acquired some formal training at the Minneapolis School of Art, and also developed his talent for cartoons. In 1969 this translated into Dave Bell's series for McMullin Publishing - the *Jock. E. Shift* cartoon which appeared in the back of *Custom Chopper* magazine. Later he produced the *Henry Hirise* cartoon for *Street Rodder* magazine and *Nat Moodle* for *Custom Rodder*.

Dave is that rare thing - an artist whose range encompasses flaming, striping, air-brushing and hand painted skills as well as cartoon work. This has given him a unique position across a whole range of auto art cultures, and allows him to cross-fertilize the influences.

When it comes to striping, however, he is most recognised for his "Old Skool" style.

Right: Dave Bell looking cool in the early 1960s.

David Hightower

Born in Pittsburgh, Kansas, David Hightower began pinstriping in high school in the 1950s. By the early '60s he had started striping professionally, emulating the Von Dutch style as practiced by Andy Southard Jr, while also spending a lot of time as a flagman at the local drag racing strip. Being part of the drag scene allowed him to work on some great cars: "I added some stripes to Swamp Rat 10, the record-breaking Don Garlits machine – it was like decorating a bat for Babe Ruth." He had a stint in the army, returned to Kansas where he worked freelance for local sign companies, got his Fine Arts degree at Pittsburgh State University in 1975, and set up shop in Lawrence, KA a year later, where he remains to this day.

Hightower soon became a recognized master at hand-lettering in particular. Then in 1991, following a Letterheads meet in Bloomington, Illinois, he realized that the panels he had used as practice could become an end in themselves. He had found his mission as an artist. And this is what he has now been most recognized for, earning the moniker "The Panel Man." He has since done hundreds, each one meticulously executed to achieve what David calls "Rock and Roll Quality." He sticks to his Old School techniques –"no computers" – and likes to describe himself as "a back porch painter."

The work says otherwise. Hightower has developed many original techniques, using foam rollers to get a dappled brush effect, or color-blending using just brushes. The backgrounds are always very carefully applied, often on a masonite base. The designs are not set before he begins; he allows them to evolve, often working on many panels at once: "I just play with it until it feels like it's done. Sometimes I don't know when to quit, and that's the hardest part."

Now highly collectable and pretty reclusive, Hightower, while he isn't "going to get rich on this," is able to do what he loves best: just to paint. He still occasionally turns his hand to striping cars and bike tanks. He is generous with his praise of other auto artists: "Glen Weisberger of Edison, New Jersey and Alton Gillepsie in Fort Worth, Texas are exceptional," but when it comes to pure panel work, Hightower is pretty much in a league of his own.

Above (main picture): David Hightower striping in the late '50s. **Above (inset):** Classic Hightower design on the trunk of a '50s Chevy.

Right: Yosemite Sam with a striped painting.

Yosemite Sam

Born in Detroit, Sam Radoff started striping at car shows when he was 12, setting up a stall where he would stripe chunky "Buddy Holly" 1950s glasses and wallets.

He took the classic route into custom painting on cars, then fabricating custom motorbikes and choppers, creating a distinct look with the latter that became influential. To date he has built nearly 1,000 custom hand-made choppers.

Nicknamed "Yosemite" for his ability to chop and paint cars, Sam's skills won him widespread recognition. His work has since featured in countless publications and the striping on his cars has won many North American show awards, including "Best of Show," "Best Paint," "Best Graphics," and "Best use of Color." In 1975 he won America's Most Beautiful Chopper award, and in 1984 *Hot Rod Magazine*'s Street Car of the Year award. He also won the Von Dutch inaugural Hall of Fame award.

Sam has always seen his striping as an art form and sees himself as an artist whose concerns stretch across media. This was recognized early when the Museum of Modern Art in Zurich, Switzerland, purchased one of his bikes for $18,000. In 1982 he moved to Ontario, Canada, and looked for new inspiration in sculpture. Today his work is featured in public spaces in London, Ontario.

This cross-fertilization has seen Sam sell pinstriped panels as domestic art. He doesn't like the categorization that comes with the art establishment, and remains true to his early affection for cars.

Today he is giving back as much as he can. There are the frequent displays at car shows, particularly in Michigan, and he has created an award to recognize the work of those involved in automobile nostalgia.

It was Sam whom Chrysler chose to promote the launch of its PT Cruiser in Canada, making him the first striper to have his work featured in a national print and TV campaign. It isn't the ultimate accolade, but telling of his stature in the world of custom paint.

USA

Alan Johnson

"I'm a car nut; when I clean a car off to stripe it, I know by the way the car is built where the stripes should go."

The perfectionist par excellence, Alan Johnson says of his works: "They're never any good. The next one is the best, always. They're always almost there." Hard to believe from the kid from Redbank who started Kustom painting in 1958, aged 12.

It was a green Ed Roth car at a show in the New York Coliseum that got him going. He started striping anything – even water skis. Then he went to the Newark School of Art, followed by a "real" job at a New York ad agency. He hated it, hated living in the City, so his wife Judy said "Why don't you just quit, go do something you love?"

That's when he opened "Alan Johnson Graphic Studios" (abbreviated to Graphix when he started losing patience on the phone) and his reputation took off. His massive body of work speaks for itself, its quality unsurpassed. His style constantly switches, from very contrasting colors to calm and mellow; it all depends on the context. He likes to "read" his customers: "I use quite a bit of psychology." But he will never do the same thing twice.

Alan is hard-working: "I get up at five and listen to classical music in the morning...and then jazz...but if I'm into some massively cool graphic I'll turn on some louder rock. Music is a big influence."

He still thinks the Pinhead movement of '92 and '93 was the best thing – and he maintains the network of contacts he acquired then. Why does he love his art so much? "The stuff in art galleries is crap. All the artwork on the road is our canvas and it's the best gallery there is. It is the renaissance of art for generations to come."

Right: Tuckered out after a hard day's work.

Opposite Page: Johnson's panel art "Lust."

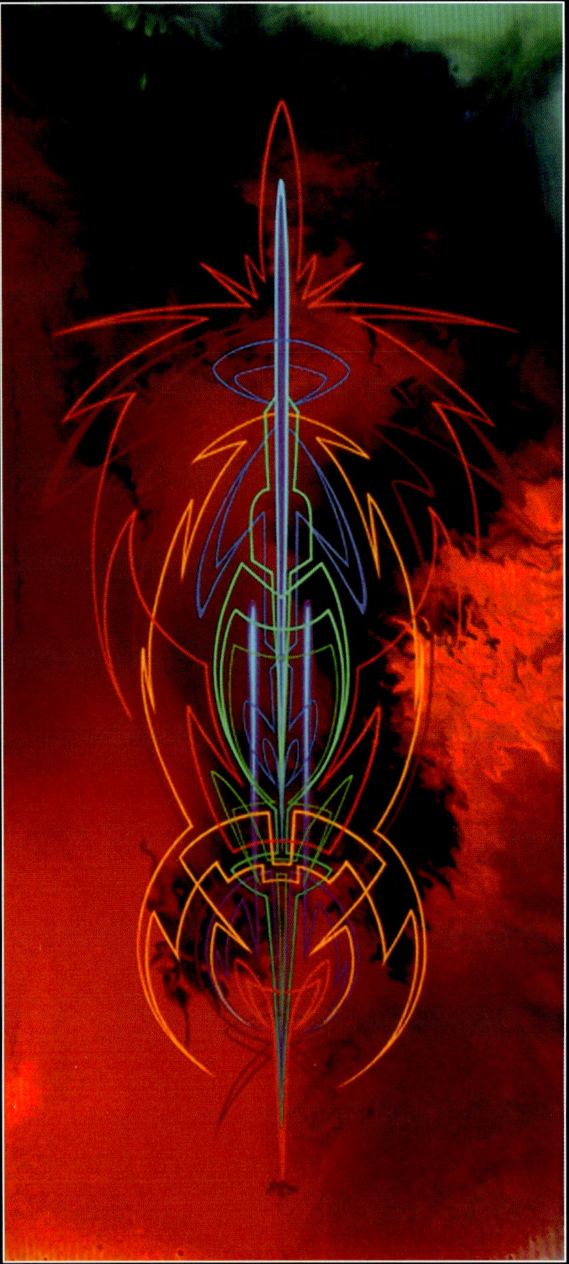

Left: "Sparks."
Right: "Wink of an Eye."

Sign Painters'
COLORFUL
HISTORY

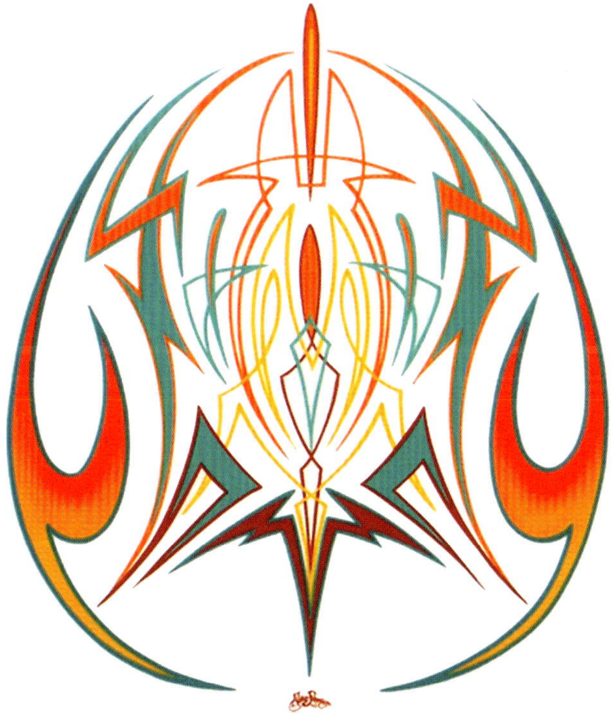

Opposite Page: "Sign Painters Colorful History."

Top Left: "Reflections of Yesterday." **Top Right:** "Southwest."
Bottom Left: "V-8 ball." **Bottom Right:** "Eagle Feather."

Craig Fraser

"Ed Roth once told me I needed a nickname...to stand out from the crowd. I figure not having one makes me stand out enough!"

Top: Craig Fraiser with Kal Koncepts Air Syndicate logo in 2004.

Page Oppostite: Gold metal flaked tank with stripes.

Finishing up someone else's pinstriping job got Craig thinking that he might have striping talent: "that undone stripe job looked so bad. I just slashed it out and thereby created the infamous slash stripe." That was in '93, and Craig hasn't looked back.

He is a classic individualist, who collaborates extensively but refuses to be pigeonholed: "I am just a Kustom painter who happens to pinstripe. I have never been a member of the Pinheads, or any other club for that matter."

The early influences were Von Dutch, Jimmy C, Herb Martinez, Bob Bond and Ron Beam. Now it's everything that he sees in the industry and beyond: "I currently take inspiration from artforms, techniques far removed from pinstriping...too much inter-industry influence tends to make the style inbred."

Craig has spent most of his life in California but lived for a year in Florence, Italy. His workshop – Air Syndicate Inc. in Bakersfield, CA – doesn't just stripe, but also paints murals and design graphics, what Craig calls his "Triple Threat." He shows at the major Kustom Kulture venues: CoproNason, La Luz De Jesus, Mary Karnoski, and at the major shows – SEMA, Coast Kustom Kulture Party, Mooneyes and the Blessing of the Cars.

And the work he's most proud of? "Probably the bike "Superstition" for John Kosmoski and the '57 Chevy wagon we painted for Jesse James." Most of all he loves the art – and the fact that the techniques and tools have changed very little in the past 200 years: "I honestly hope it doesn't change – nice to know some things stay the same."

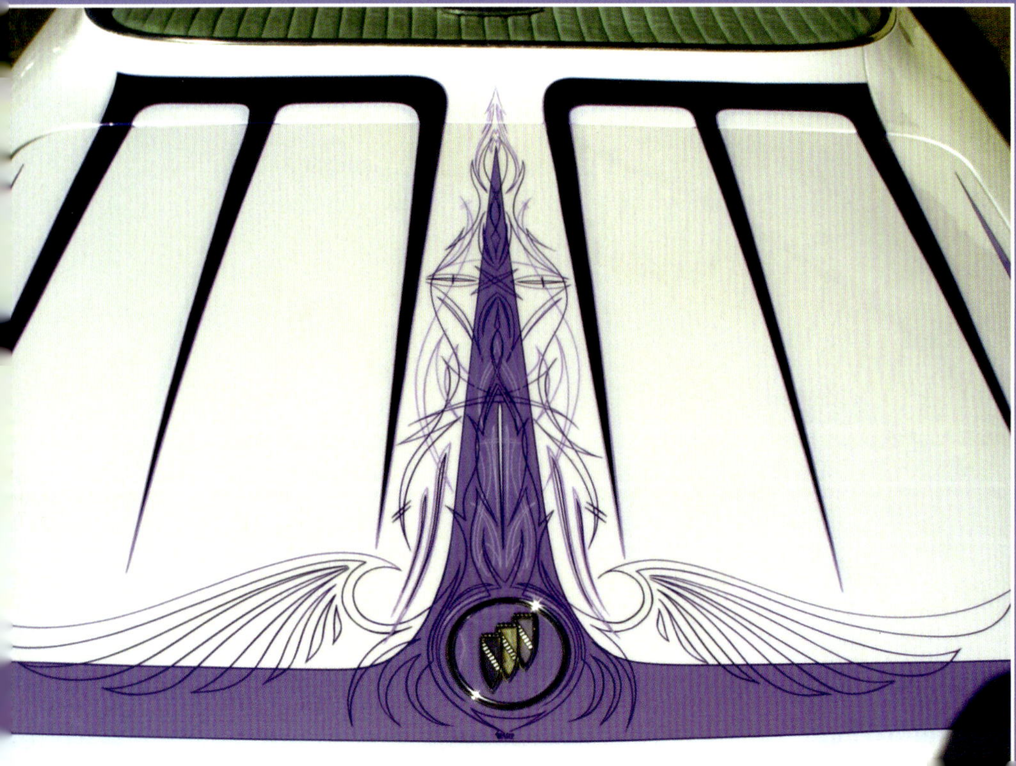

Left and Right: Craig Fraser by his '61 Buick Le Sabre, with his description of the car below.

This 1961 Buick LeSabre was purchased by Craig Fraser in 1998, from the original owner. It retains the factory 368 Wildcat motor, and all drivetrain remains stock. The entire car is kustom painted with various shades of violet kandy, and pinstriped with lavender, violet, and white pinstriping. The car is nicknamed 'Devil, or Angel,' and has won the best scallop award, and best pinstriping at the KOA Paso Robles show. It has been featured in Club International magazine, as well as Hot Rod magazine.

The chrome trim and bumpers are all original. The rims are Supremes, with Coker white walls. The front and rear suspension has been airbagged, and will lower and raise 6 inches, with full suspension provided by outboard mounted gas shocks on the front a-arms and the rear load leveller mounts. The ride is better than factory, and looks a hell of a lot kewler.

It has Von Dutch style pinstriping on the decks. The roof is violet kandy metalflake, and the entire paint job has a layer of "Purple Haze" pearl throughout the clear.

Even the dash is kustom painted, with freehand airbrushed Kustom Kulture artwork. The interior is all violet and white tuck-n-roll, with a violet metal flake steering wheel and tiki shifter. The stereo has been updated with a CD player and 500 watts of Orion power, and Lansar speakers. All hidden from view.

KONCEPTS
833-8486
KUSTOM PAINT
KUSTOMS GONE BAD
KGB
APPAREL & ARTWORK
RACING
SYNDICATE
836-3084
KUSTOM AIRBRUSH
AIR SYND

OUTLAW
OUTLAW

FRASER
SPAUN

This Page: Craig painting various aspects of "Stray Cat" drag racer, including skull and crossed wrenches and Craig's "Kal Koncepts" autograph mark.

Opposite Page Top: Craig putting finishing touches to the fender of the "Outlaw" bike.
Opposite Page Bottom: Front and rear view of striped round box.

"Dirty" Donny Gillies

"From an early age I was fascinated with monsters, cars and Rock 'n' Roll. I even kustomised my radio flyer with spray paint and a carpet; I was 4."

Top: Donny chowing down at Whizz Burger. (Photo courtesy of Jamin Barton)

"Dirty" Donny Gillies was thrust upon an unsuspecting world on March 4th, 1974 in Ottawa, Canada. His early fascination with cartoons, comic books and model kits led directly to Donny withdrawing into his own self-created world of monsters and hot rods. Unfortunately, his early creativity went unappreciated and he was deemed a problem student, so he dropped out of school at the tender age of 14 and never looked back. Ironically, the "bad kid" image worked to his advantage in the punk rock scene, where he further cut his teeth designing endless flyers, demo tape covers and eventually LP jackets. As a result of this 'baptism of fire' he can paint, draw and build things like nobody's business. This led to commissions doing large silk-screened posters and CD covers for bands like New Jersey's infamous Electric Frankenstein, the Swedish sensation The Hellacopters, The Wildhearts from the UK and Japan's The 5.6.7.8's, where his now in-demand style was a perfect fit.

His profile as a commercial artist has recently been further raised by having his artwork grace the covers of magazines like *AMP*, *Lollipop*, *Carbon 14*, and *Gearhead*, and through features in *International Tattoo Art* and *Metal Hammer* as well as weeklies like *San Francisco Bay Guardian*, *The Montreal Mirror*, *The Ottawa Citizen* and *Rust and Drive*. He has appeared in countless group shows including the successful *Everything But The Kitchen Sink* show at the La Luz de Jesus gallery in Los Angels, *Tag The System* in NYC as well as the *Sci-fi Western* show in San Francisco. Currently Donny has been commissioned by Metallica to do no less than fifteen separate jobs for them, everything from painting large murals in their rehearsal space, to designing their guitar picks and a new T-shirt, to pinstriping a grand piano, some of which can be seen in the motion picture *Some Kind Of Monster*. Donny has also worked as in-house artist for Gearhead Records and has recently signed on with Poster Pop who now feature his original creations on stickers, T-shirts, and patches. His "God of 3-D" design was the first sticker in Poster Pop's 10-year history to sell out almost immediately. Whatever the future holds for this undeniably talented artist, it promises to be interesting.

Top: One of Dirty Donny's sticker designs for Poster Pop: "Buckethead."
Bottom: Dirty Donny has a thing about striping toolboxes – here is one example for Metallica HQ .

Top: Striped USS Bumbeck II BBQ .
Above: Design for Poster Pop sticker "66 Sick."

Top: Another striped toolbox, this time for Paul.
Middle: "Four Eyes" toilet seat.
Bottom: Yet another striped toolbox, for Larry.
Above Right: Design for "Skate Monster" Poster Pop sticker .

Above: Several shots and detail of Danny's "Magic Nose Goblin" bicycle. As Danny says, "Rolling slow is cool, and so is eating boogers."

GMC

Herb Martinez

"I always wanted to be a custom painter. I focused on it when I was 13 years old."

Top: Herb striping a thin white line above a previous striped red line at the European Street Rod Nationals, Weilburg, Germany, 2006.

Opposite Page: Limited edition print on white parchment.

Born in San Francisco in 1946, Herb's family moved to Oakland when he was five. Oakland provided fertile ground for his active imagination. His first mentor, Doug Dilley, lived next door with his '53 Studebaker decorated by Von Dutch. He taught Herb how to use a striping brush; Herb's mum then bought Herb his first brush, a Grumbaker.

Herb remembers riding his bike around Oakland as a teenager, bumping into Tommy the Greek – "he was unselfish in letting me learn whilst looking over his shoulder." He looked up another Oakland resident – "St John" Morton at Red Lee's Automotive Artists' Shop. "I was lucky to meet such willing teachers – in those days there was a lot of secrecy around techniques."

After serving his country in the Navy, Herb met Cary Greenwood, and it was thanks to him that he made the jump from normal car and custom painting into full-time striping. By 1970 he had opened his "Color Machine" paint shop in Oakland, specialising in motorcycles and race cars.

Adopting the nickname "The Line Doctor" Herb is now based in Livermore CA. He's an active member of the NHRA, Rod and Custom Association and Goodguys. As a member of SEMA he tours nationally and internationally (to date Japan, Germany and Switzerland) demonstrating his art.

Every major hot rod publication has featured Herb's work, and he has worked for the major Hollywood movie studios – including 20th Century Fox, Lions Gate and Universal.

"I am now not just a practioner – I am also the classic student-turned-teacher: it's about passing the tradition on to a new generation" he says.

35/50

Ford

MUSTANG
WRJ 878

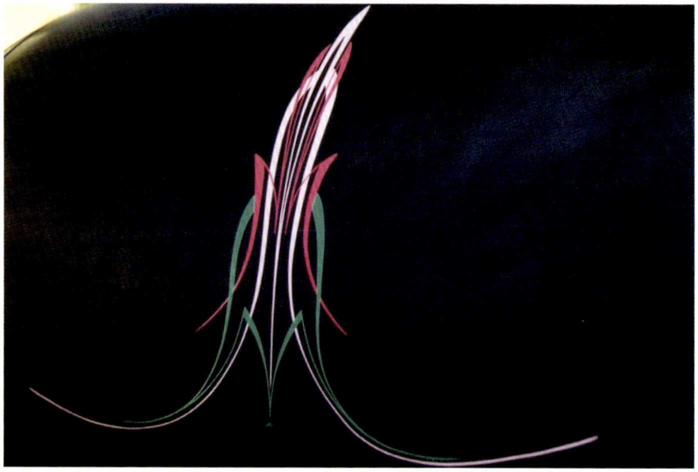

LRGJ810

RECARO

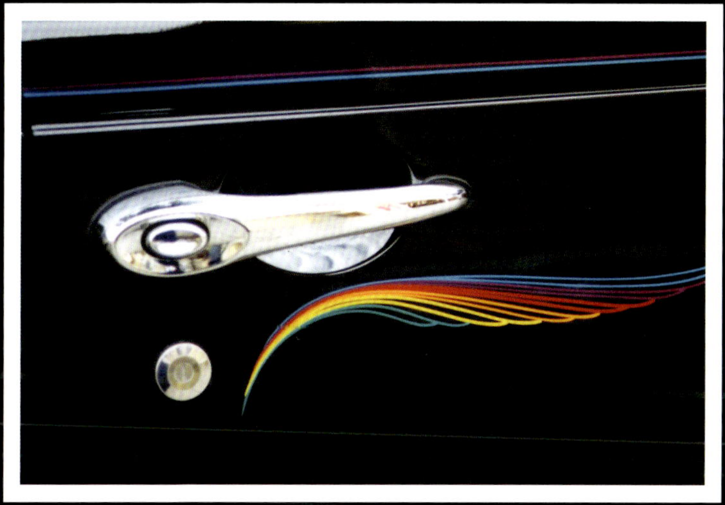

Opposite Page:
Top Left and Right: Herb: "My first experience seeing pinstriping done was the work of Tommy the Greek. His signature teardrops and 1/4 inch accent lines and scallops were synonymous with the style of customs and hot rods from the San Francisco area in the 1950s and '60s."

Middle Left, Right and Bottom Left: Herb: "One design begets another. In this three picture example of how one style works into other designs, the first design on the water truck is changed by adding a thick to thin line design. The basic design itself still remains the same but is widened to allow the thick/thin lines to have room to look aesthetically correct. The third picture shows the addition of a center "art nouveau" design with the thick to thin lines accenting it."

Bottom Right: Herb: "Sponge flames have been a mainstay for me in the last 5 or so years. Most of the work has been done on PT Cruisers. This Mitsubishi Eclipse was done for a book on building "fast and furious" style vehicles and combines both graphics and flames."

This Page:
Top Left and Right, and Bottom Left: Herb: "Dry brush style graphics were great for any car. This style was popular in the 1990s and is still somewhat popular now."

Bottom Right: Herb: "This style of design is called a "feather." My main mentor, Cary Greenwood, taught me this design and we used it thousands of times on conversions of vans."

Jimmy C

"The Kustom Scene is spreading around the world, growing like crazy. There's no end in sight!"

As a kid Jimmy C moved around, all over New Mexico and Arizona: "My Dad was a heavy equipment operator, building roads. By the time I was one, we had lived in 9 different towns." It stayed that way for Jimmy C until high school.

Jimmy remembers how everyone was into bikes and vans when he was a kid, and the magazines that followed the trend : "They featured wild paint jobs you could only dream about." His fate was pretty much sealed on going to work his first day at Michael B's sign shop. He walked in on Michael lettering and striping a race car: "I just fell in love with what he was doing."

Two years later, having learnt from Mike, Jimmy opened his first sign shop. His first "Rat Fink" party in California was formative, seeing the work of stripers from all over the world. "It was there that I met Ed "Big Daddy" Roth, one of my childhood heroes. The inspiration was huge...my world was never the same."

Jimmy sees how computers have changed some approaches to pinstriping, but as he puts it: "With a bit of enamel, a striping sword, and a lettering quill the possibilities are endless."

He is not just a major contributor to the Kustom Kulture scene in the US and beyond. He see his art as a continuation of a much older tradition: "Sign painting and the embellishment that comes with it is the oldest trade in the world. It will always be around – the modern age can't take that away. It will become a more and more valuable art form."

Below: Jimmy C striping the underside of a surfboard.

Opposite Page: Tiki-inspired "Crazy Guy" painting.

JimmyC 98'

Above: Postcard promoting Jimmy C's sculpted fiberglass bodies of Ed "Big Daddy" Roth's original 1958 "Outlaw." **Right:** More examples of Jimmy C's Tiki obsessions: oil drum and panel artwork.

Opposite Page: Another Jimmy C Tiki-inspired painting.

JimmyC 98'

This Page and Opposite:
Jimmy C's RV (with Labrador) showing striped hood, side panels flamed with tribal design, and Jimmy's autograph mark. The RV was a former airport shuttle van. Jimmy took out all the seats, put on the bubble top, and painted it all up.

JimmyC
SAN CLEMENTE, CALIF.

Mr. J

"As a kid, much to my parents' dismay, I'd stripe anything I could lay my hands on, including quite a bit of furniture."

Julian "Mr. J" Braet got into hot rod culture very early, from consuming everything he read in car magazines. He also became an avid buyer of books on the subject: "I had at my fingertips work done by the masters in California."

After graduating from high school, he met a sign artist called Tony Anthony. "He was a great teacher and he agreed to let me apprentice in his shop. It was a great education. I am really grateful for the opportunity."

In 1960 Mr. J opened his own shop in Newark, NJ, specializing in airbrush lettering and pinstriping. While being influenced by the classic masters – Ed "Big Daddy" Roth, Von Dutch, Dean Jeffries, Larry Watson and Tommy the Greek – Mr. J began developing a distinctive style, which became recognized as the "Jersey Look" in graphics.

Mr. J has also been a significant figure within the industry. "I like to get involved not just in writing magazines, but also by doing practical demos at the international and national trade shows, and at letterhead and pinhead events." He has also gotten involved in designing tools and brushes for stripe artists, through his Excalibur Corp. company.

"I've been in this business now for over 25 years and one thing I've learnt is that secrecy about techniques and tricks doesn't advance things. I like to share these. I want to help everyone become the best in their craft."

Opposite Page: Mr. J's Von Dutch tribute. Artwork, metal panel painted matte black, with striping and classic Von Dutch flying eyeball motif.

Von Dutch
U.S.A

24B

MERCURY
New Jersey

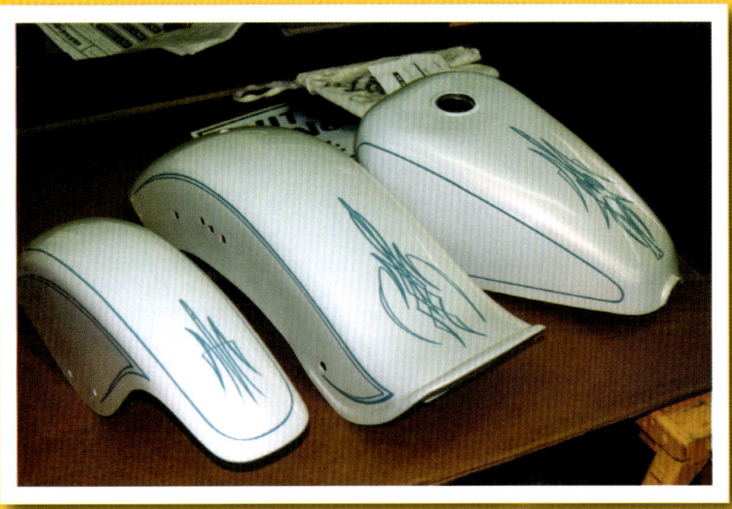

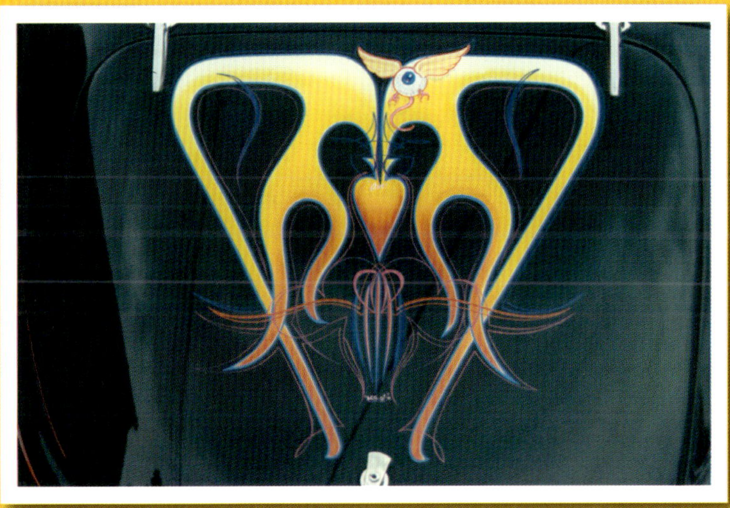

Opposite Page:
Top Left: 2 color enamel pinstriping around '53 Ford custom car.
Top Right: Antique car with body lines outlined and designs done in enamel.
Mid Left: Hood of '53 Ford custom striped in 2 color enamel.
Mid Right: Fiberglass bodied "Legend" race car. Airbrush lettering, striping and graphics in enamel.
Bottom Right: '50 Merc custom deck lid striped in 2 colors using enamel.
Bottom Left: Same Merc with striping around the sunken antenna.

This Page:
Top Left: Pearl white motorcycle parts, striped in blue-green enamel.
Top Right: Motorcycle front fender striped in 23 karat gold leaf. Striping in enamel, in parts clear-coated.
Mid Left: Deck lid of '37 Ford hot rod, with flames, striping & art work in enamel.
Bottom Left: Racing helmet in enamel.
Bottom Right: Striping on hood of '50 Ford custom car.

All pinstriping done with Mr. J's Xcaliber brushes; lettering & graphics done with brown quills & flats. Airbrushing done with "Iwata Eclipse."
Paint: Roanan lettering enamels.

Ryzart

"Pinstriping is in essence a simple art, yet so hard to master; the visuals are so complex, yet instantly pleasing to the eye."

One of the youngest skilled pinstripers around, Ryzart may only be 28 years old but he has already shown at the classic venues - Kustom Kulture Gallery in NYC, the Gasoline Gallery and Victoria Studios in L.A., and Detroit Autorama.

Born in New Jersey (and still based there), Ryzart started drawing as soon as he could pick up a pencil.

He aspired to be a comic book artist but, after two years of formal graphics training, decided that "my drawing skills were not up to par." Then, following one of those pinstriping demo conversion moments at a car show, he turned to striping as a way to express his art. The early influences – Von Dutch and Ed "Big Daddy" Roth – are complemented by more recent inspiration including California's Craig Fraser and Makoto from Japan.

"I will stripe anything!" declares Ryzart. The range of his work proves it: amongst his commissions are Garwood Fire Dept, Snap-Action, Full Arsenal, Frank 151, Mayhem Custom Cycles, and Rumblers Car Club.

Ryzart's take on striping is reaching an ever wider audience. His work is regularly shown in Kustom Kulture magazines such as *Burnout*, *Ol Skool Rodz* and *Airbrush Action*; he also shows on the Fuse cable channel. "I am totally addicted to striping!" he says. "I'm constantly learning new techniques and developing the art."

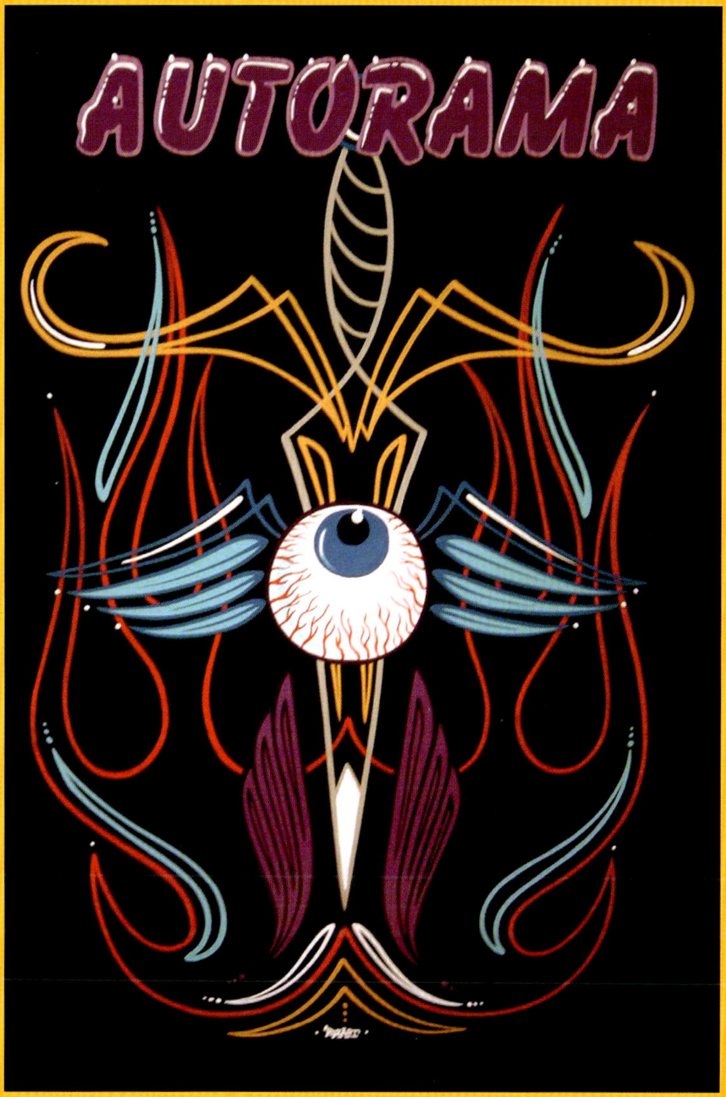

Above: Panel art for Detroit Autorama.
Left: Striped and flamed coffee table.

Opposite Page Top from Left: "Mom" artwork, evoking classic tattooing; "Kustom Vulture;" and "Shrunken Head" with Tiki overtones.

This Page: Striping on bike fenders and gas tanks.

Opposite Page:
Top: "Good Luck 13" wooden panel, with painted cuthroat razors.
Middle: Shrunken head with cuthroat razors and spider's web.
Right: Tiki snowboard.

13
GOOD LUCK

Skratch

"I wasn't born. I was fabricated."

Above: Skratch striping a helmet with 1 Shot paint.

Born in Texas, to a mother who painted in the classical style, and a father who created pen-and-ink hot rod art, it is not surprising that Skratch (his legal name), ended up pursuing the path he has.

As a teen, Skratch built and raced custom cars, and somehow ended up doing a stint at General Motors. Skratch's early talent was for two-handed pinstriping. Under the apprenticeship of Frank Palmer he perfected the craft. An early love for Von Dutch's work led Skratch to become the in-house striper for Von Dutch Originals in L.A.: on arrival in the City, he laid claim to his new territory by striping the parking meters down Melrose Avenue.

The gig at Von Dutch did not last for long, however, as Skratch had too great a sense of independence, and the urge for creative freedom was strong. In 2002 Skratch started his own empire, in the form of Skratch's Garage.

The shop cemented Skratch's reputation as one of the best sign painters and stripers in the business. His style is characterized by great composition and sharp, clean, and balanced line work. Like Von Dutch, Skratch is also uncompromising to the point of obstinacy. He believes in the uniqueness of each work and refuses to do the same thing twice. His friendship with 'artist-at-large' Dennis McPhail was a major influence: "He challenged me to grow creatively and to seriously pursue graphics."

In a few short years, Skratch has built an enviable reputation. His clients now include Barris Customs, *The O.C.*, the Garage Company, and Tyler Surfboards. His artwork has been seen in New York City galleries, and in the Hollywood feature films *Dragnet* and *View From The Top*. He has been covered in over 20 automotive, motorcycle and sports magazines worldwide, including *Burnout, Ol Skool Rodz*, *Rod & Custom*, and *Car Kulture Deluxe*. He has contributed to TLC's "Overhauling" with its three-time Ridler Award-winning host Chip Foose (on the 1952 GMC Truck, the '70 Camaro, and the Double Hauling episodes). Skratch was also the narrator of the Kustom Kulture documentary *Back from the Dead*.

Skratch's work is a fixture of the scene, thanks to his regular appearances at the annual Mooneyes BBQ, the Rat Fink Extravaganza, Viva Las Vegas, The World Art Show, Tokyo Groovy, the Antique Nationals, KOA, and the Paso Robles West Coast Customs Car Show. And he's still only 29.

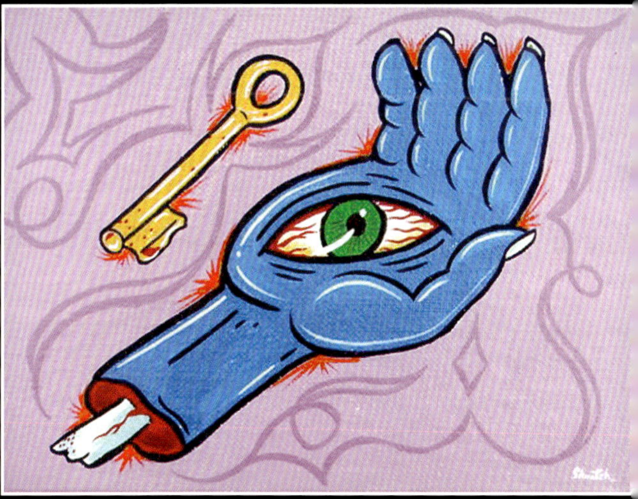

Top Left: "Skull and Wrench" original artwork. 1 Shot paint on canvas.
Top Right: "Heart and Skull" original artwork. 1 Shot on canvas, for Steel Clothing, Japan, 2004.

Above: "Hand" original artwork with striping, 2005. 1 Shot on canvas.
Left: "Barbie," 2004. 1 Shot on Barbie doll. Private collection.

Opposite Page: Skratch focusing hard on the job at hand.
This page: The brilliant end result.

Tony Perez

"When I was a kid there was a Chinese restaurant next door: some customers were surprised when they came out after a meal to find their cars had been striped."

Tony Perez grew up in Phoenix, Arizona with cars in his blood. His dad's custom paint and fabrication shop would do "Everything: chop tops, French antennas, suicide doors and custom painting." His Dad showed him a few techniques and Tony's future as a master pinstriper was written: "Pinstriping is addictive once you start practicing. It is hard to put the brush down."

The paintshop was on Central Avenue in downtown Phoenix, where people would come to cruise their cars and bikes on Friday and Saturday nights. Tony used to paint on those evenings – street rods, low-riders and bikes. And his designs and techniques got better and better.

When he turned 18, Tony joined the Marines to see the world and chose Okinawa as his first posting. "I took my brushes and album to a local body shop and they really liked what they saw in the pictures. I would go out and stripe a few cars every time I got the chance." On his tour of duty Tony left examples of his work in Korea, Singapore, Hong Kong, Thailand, the Philippines, and Kenya.

He started his renowned business, Pinstripes by Tony, in '87, and developed a website, www.pinstriper.com, to provide advice to new stripers. He has since shown at all the major shows, and has developed a close relationship with the Von Dutch stores in Milan, Florence, Rome, and London.

The big influences? Well his Dad for one, but also Von Dutch and Ed Roth. He still gets a buzz from striping late into the night "30 years from when I started - some things never change." The work he is most proud of is the recent stuff on bikes: "I always look forward to the next challenge," he says.

Right: Tony striping a hand-carved statue by California-based Tiki Bosko.

Opposite Page: T-shirt design with flying eye motif for Pinstriper.com.

©TONY
WWW.PINSTRIPER.COM

Above: Tony Perez striping the window of the Von Dutch store in Rome, Italy.

Opposite Page: Group shot of Tony's retro gas pumps for Von Dutch stores, often converted to be used as display cabinets.

HIGH OCTANE
SO-CAL
SPEED SHOP
FORD-MERCURY
SERVICE
HIGH OCTANE
Von Dutch
ORIGINALS
HIGH OCTANE DRINKS
Von Dutch
ORIGINALS

This Page: Tony Perez's lettering and striping for Goldman's Salt Track racer.

Top: Custom retro ivory flames pinstriped in red on a '50s pickup for Matt Weidma at Roadside Relics.
Bottom: This black and orange truck is Tony Perez's daily driv an 02 Dakota done in tangerine yellow, and red pearl with blac negative flames pinstriped in lime green.

This Page and Opposite: Custom Chopper "Slingshot" with candy tangerine fade to black, silver tribal graphics with lime green and process blue pinstriping. Bike custom built by Terry Lee. Photos courtesy of *Street Chopper Magazine.*

This Page and Opposite: "Streetwalker" with large silver metal flake, candy red and black graphics on top, and lime green pinstriping, built by Terry Lee of Envy Cycle Creations.

EUROPE

Empire 32

"When I first started you just couldn't get the materials in France: I had to import the paint and brushes from the US."

Obsessed with *Hot Rod Magazine* from when he was a teen, Empire 32 trained at Art School in Strasbourg, France, near the German border. Still primarily a graphic designer, he turns to striping for inspiration and fun: "Striping joins two of my passions – hot rods and Kustom and graphic art." It's hard to believe from his work that this is a part-time activity and Empire has clearly studied the techniques in depth. "I am inspired by all sorts of things, but in the world of striping I am particularly impressed by the Japanese guys and of course the pioneering Americans."

He shows his work – bikes and cars – on his website and at rockabilly weekends and car shows in Germany, Belgium and Switzerland. "My best work will always be my next one, because the goal is always to make progress; I try to use traditional pinstripe motifs and create new ones. When I start to stripe a car I don't have any predefined ideas or designs. I start with a few notions of the colors I will use and then I improvise."

Right: Empire 32 in his Strasbourg workshop with signage and panel art.

Opposite Page: Striped Panel.

E32

E32

Opposite Page: Empire 32 striped panel art, with skull motif.

This Page: Selection of Empire's striping on car trunks, car hoods and bike fenders.

Jon Leeson

"There is so much to stripe but so little time!"

Opposite Page: Stripes on distressed panel, with abstract motif.

John Leeson's father and grandfather were both signwriters who could stripe, so you could say he has it in his blood: "It was called coachlining and decoration back then, not pinstriping." As a kid, he was fascinated by the designs in *Custom Car Magazine*. "By the time I started my apprenticeship my Dad had started getting *Signcraft Magazine*, which included a pinstriping section in each issue and the whole thing just snowballed for me."

Jon (a.k.a. The Letterknight) has always lived in and around the Leicester area, about 50 miles north of London, U.K. He recently moved onto a narrow boat moored on the Ashby Canal, 25 miles west: "My boat should be finished by the end of the year and will be completely striped out, with a kind of '30s feel. Maybe striped boats will catch on; who knows ?"

His studio is characterized by the mix of work – signage, narrow boats, motor sports and road vehicles. Jon also sees striping cross-fertilizing more than ever: "Striping seems to be more mainstream – T-shirts, caps and logo designs. I also see more striping in tattoos." His own work responds to this trend. "I'm working on a series of panels that will include striping, lettering, artwork, gold and dimensional stuff, all tied together."

When it comes to influences, "There are so many," but he checks off David Hightower, Alan Johnson, Alton Gillespie, Jeff Williams, John Falotico and Neil Meillard – "He's an awesome letterer and striper." Jon attends as many Letterhead and Pinhead meets as he can – "Apart from the exchange of ideas, I've met some great people... We all have this desire to lay down the line and do our own thing."

"Striping is a big part of my life," he reflects, "And I ultimately do it for myself. It's a really good way to get my creative rocks off!"

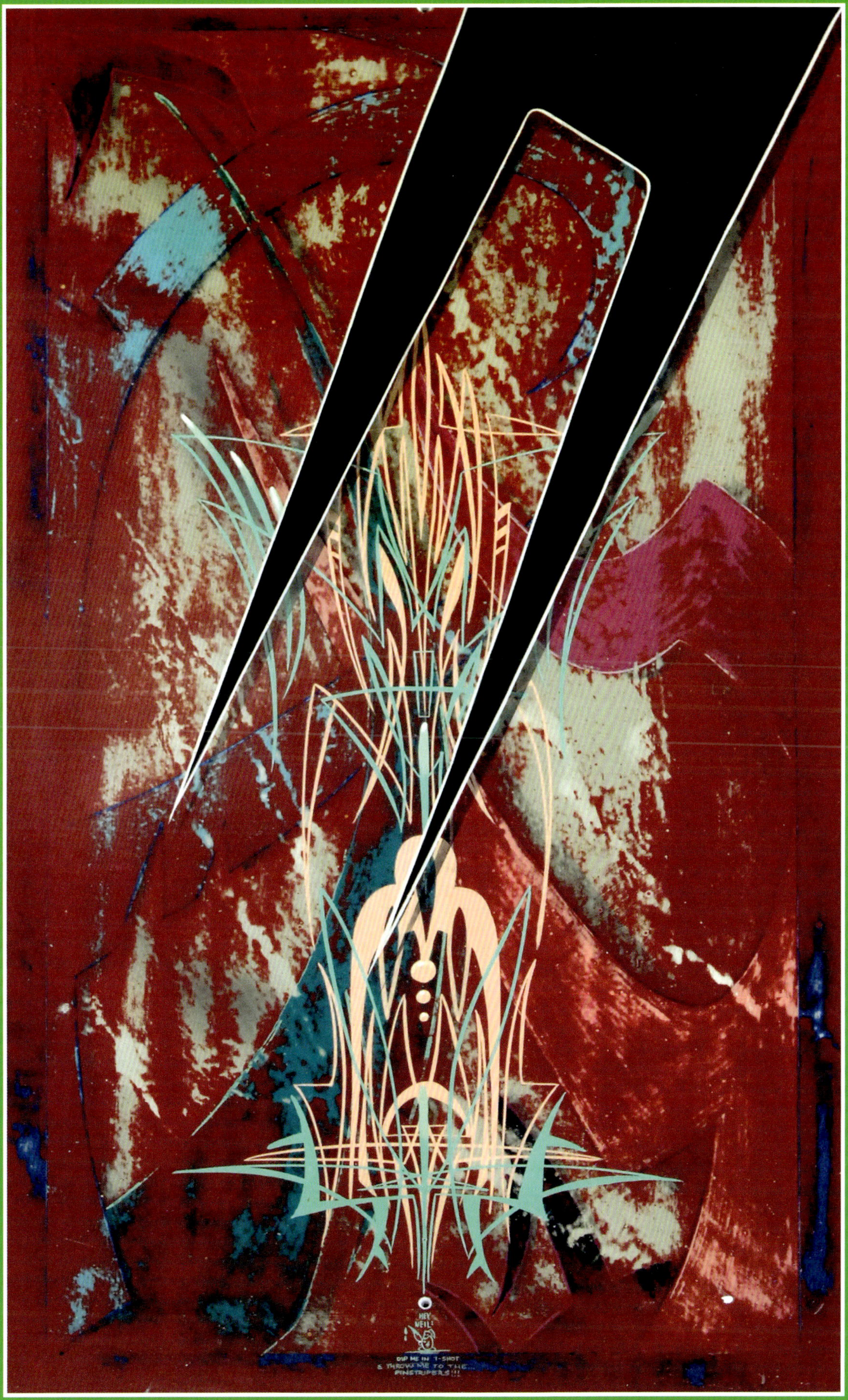
HEY NEIL!
DIP ME IN 1-SHOT
& THROW ME TO THE
PINSTRIPERS!!!

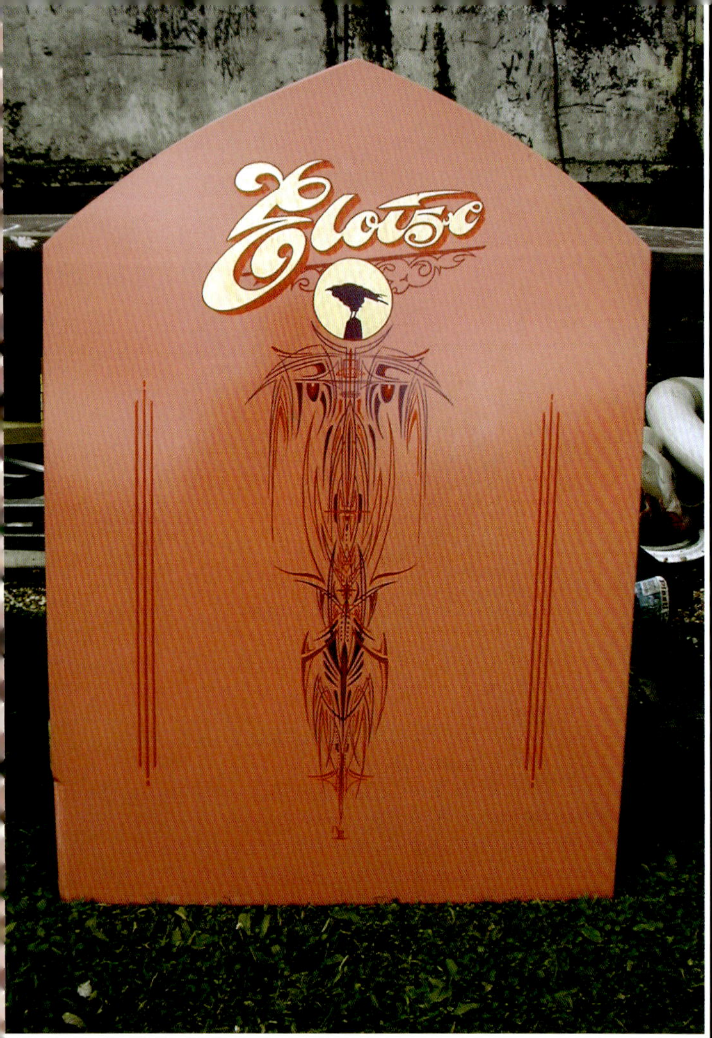

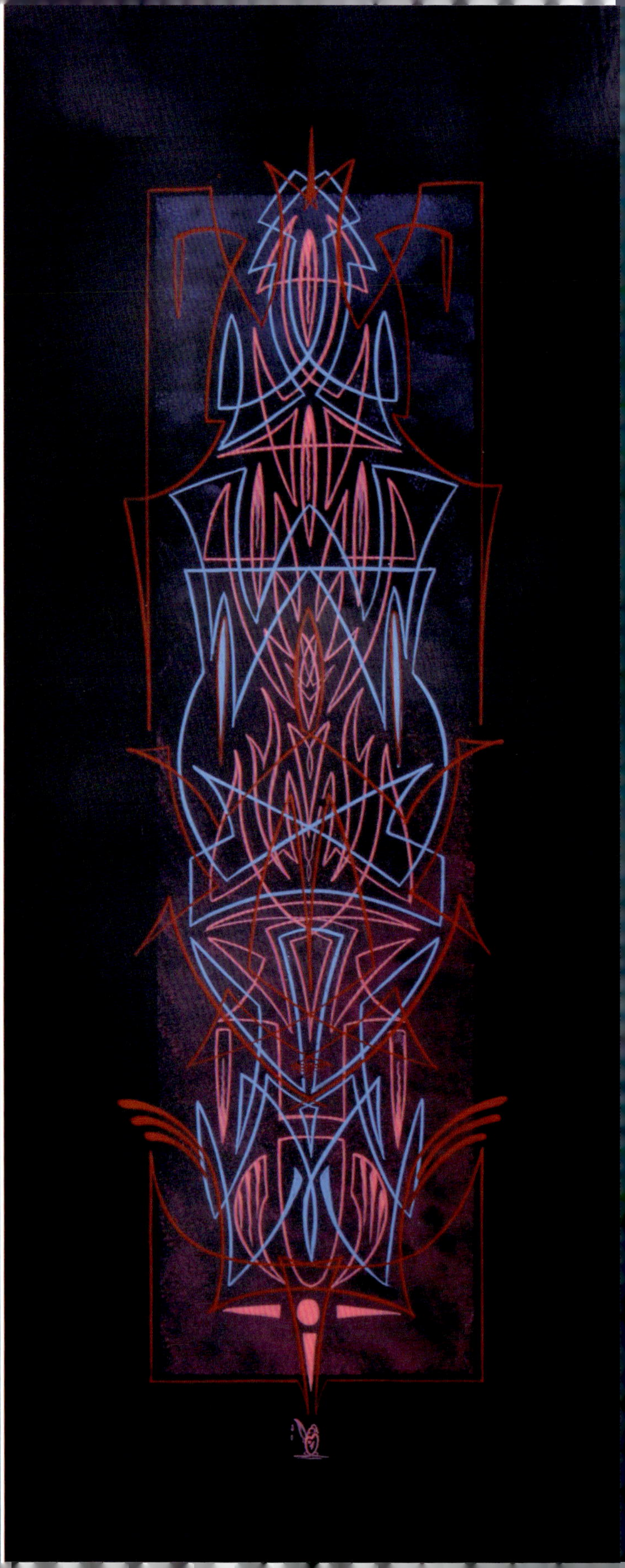

Top: "Eloise" striped gravestone shaped panel, with black crow detail.
Above: Fantasy car airbrushed art, with striped side panels.
Right: Striped panel, with Tiki overtones.

Opposite Page: "Stripers Diner" 3-D panel, with striped background detailing.

Stripers
BAR &
DINER

Maze

"The main influence for me is Von Dutch... he added so much spirit to his work... it's a great source of inspiration."

Born in Cologne, Germany in 1977, Mathias Wagner, a.k.a. Maze, was first a painter in oils and then a professional airbrusher before discovering pinstriping on a flame-outlining job. When a friend handed him an old swordstriper he became hooked, drawing inspiration from "any snippet with stripes on it." Still based in Cologne (why move from a great place?), Maze works individually as a striper, but collaborates with Jenz Fischer from Kustom Rebelz for clearcoating and with Husky Linz, who does the leatherwork on his vehicles.

For Maze, pinstriping is a way of carrying forward the great cultural heritage started in California in the 1950s. An increasing workload – "it's becoming really popular here in Germany, which is great because I have a ton of work to do" – and reputation have seen him show at major European car shows and a few bike shows too.

"I think my spraypainting may have influenced some other artists; it's probably too early to say when it comes to my pinstriping... let's wait and see," he says.

Amongst his best work is his Kustom Rebelz 1954 Ford F-100 with ghost flames and striping.

Above: Maze in King of Stripers mode, with large striped panel art in background.

Opposite Page: Examples showing range of Maze's striping work, and two examples of airbrush art.

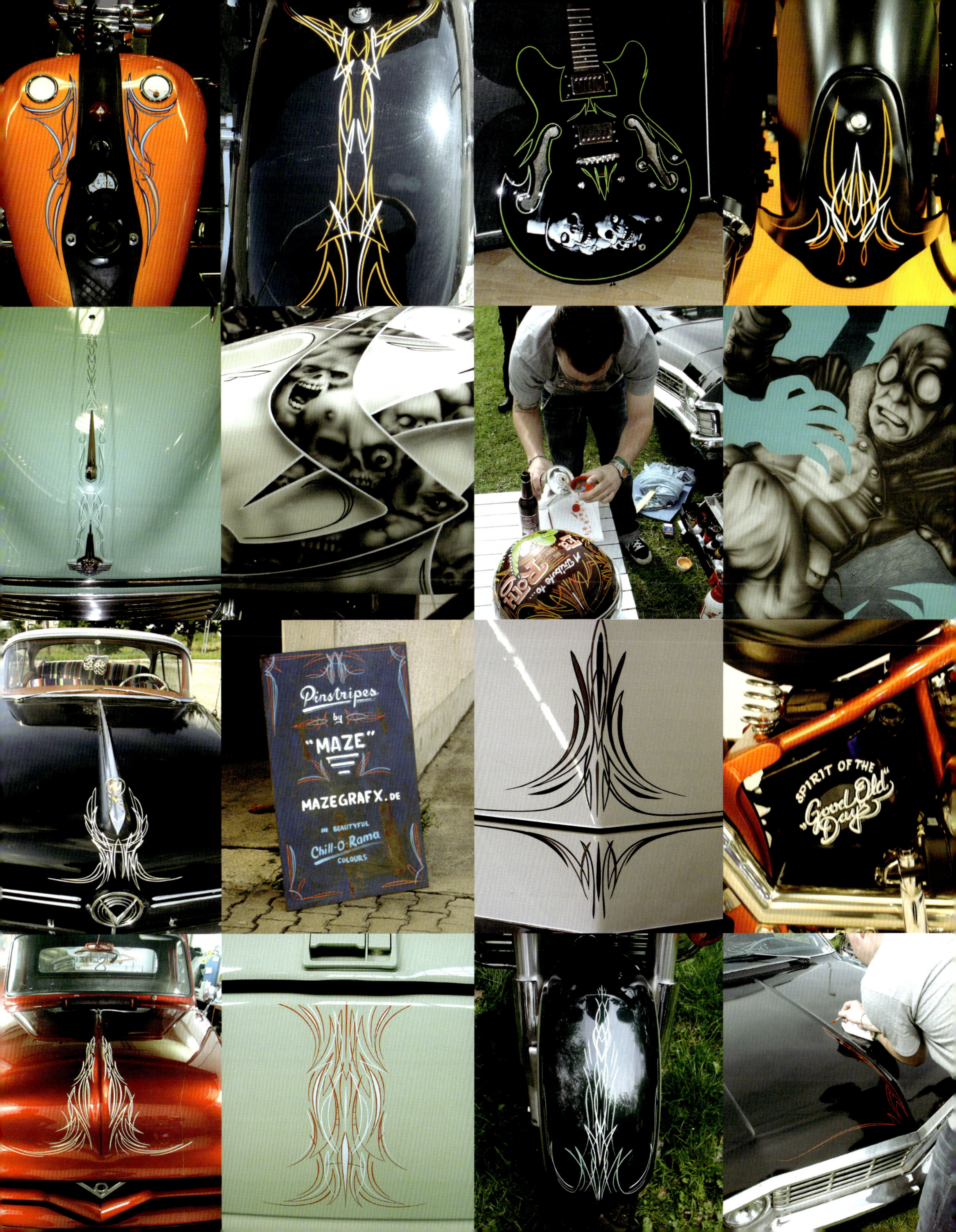
Pinstripes
by
"MAZE"
MAZEGRAFX.DE
IN BEAUTYFUL
Chill-O-Rama
COLOURS
SPIRIT OF THE
"Good Old Days"

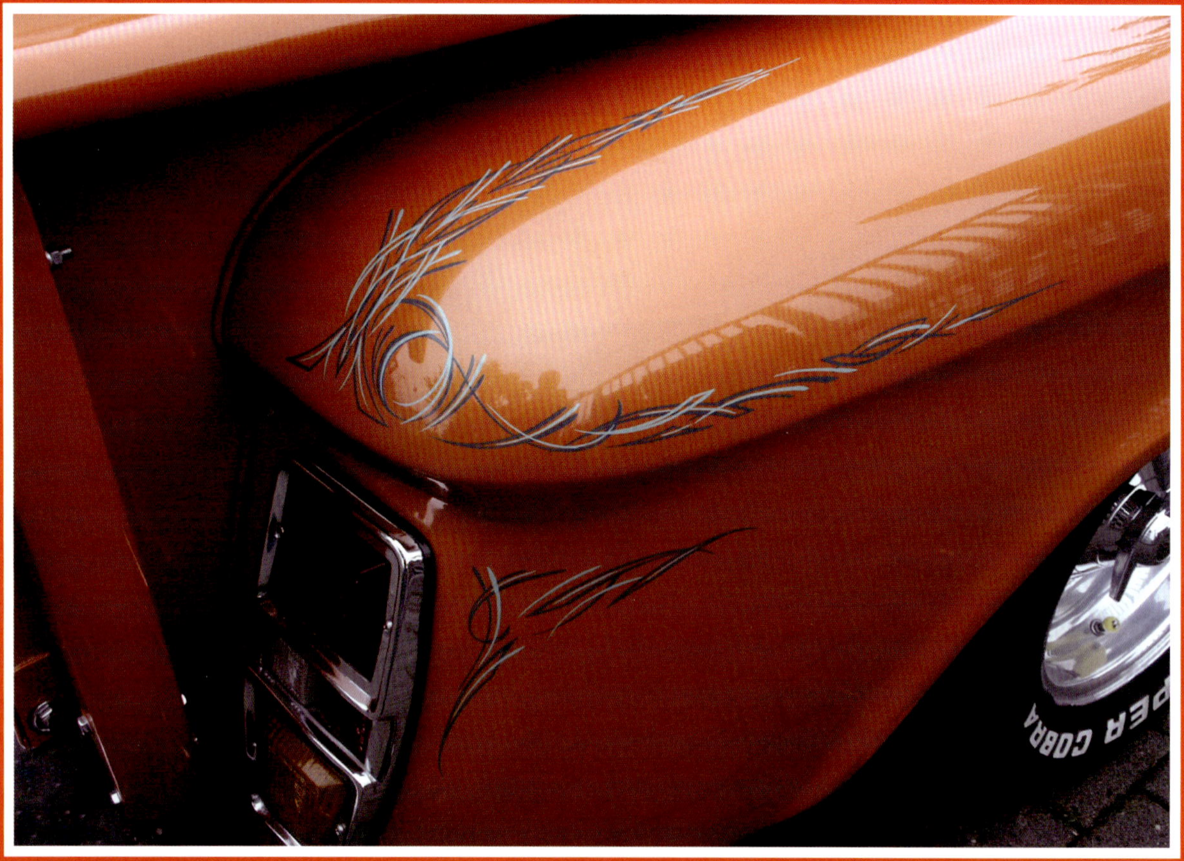

Top: Maze: "A '57 Chevy Stepside where I used mixed 1 Shot colors to match the interior and flame the hood..."
Bottom: "...and did some weird stripes everywhere else."

Opposite Page:
Top: Maze: "A nice '64 Thunderbird...amazing car to do stripes on!"
Bottom: Maze: "Some clean lines around the back couldn't be wrong here."

MOTUL

Melissa G

"I got the bug to stripe when I went to Paso Robles and saw another lady striper and thought: I could do that!"

British Melissa Gee worked for 12 years in a design studio, doing art work for major corporations, before adopting pinstriping. But it was always in her blood. From a young age she remembers her dad racing MG's and her brother acquiring a Dodge Charger; the moment she got her license at 17, Melissa bought a Ford Pop – " The beginning of a very long list of cars."

Following that moment of conversion in Paso Robles, Simon Watts (from Australia) became her main influence. She also drew inspiration from Bobbo Dunn, Steve Kafka, Butchr whom she met at the Phoenix Brush Bash, and most of all "Von Dutch, for his great talent and attitude to striping."

Melissa works individually in Doncaster, South Yorkshire, and shows mainly at Kustom bike and hot rod shows in the UK and occasionally at Viva Las Vegas. She's proud of all her work, "Including the early stuff," but singles out her husband's 1932 Truck – where even the floorpan is striped – and the lid of a '40 Merc Convertible called "El Diablo," featuring a devil's head surrounded by striping.

Melissa now has a strong following in the UK, with many newcomers asking her for lessons on how to stripe. She comments on how striping there has never been more popular, but that "there are some great stripers out there who don't get any recognition."

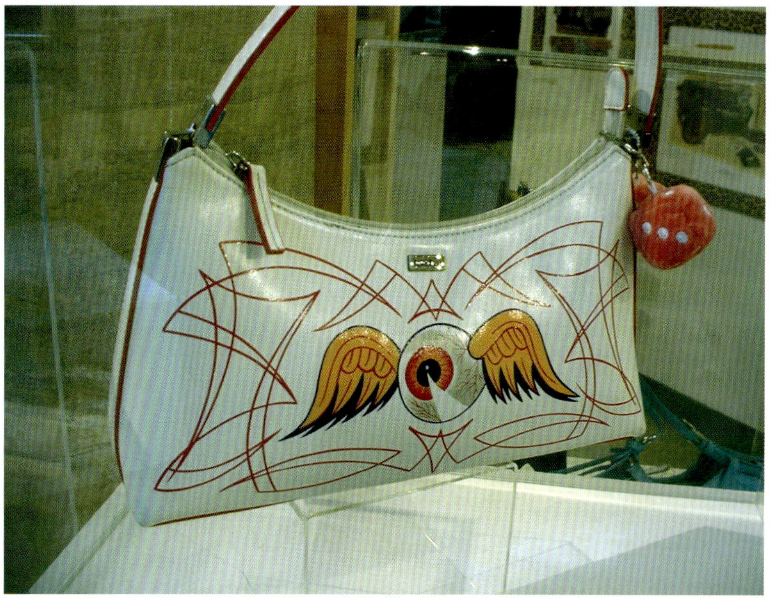

Above: A selection of Melissa's striped handbags; these examples show Tiki designs, the flying eyeball and iron cross.

Opposite Page: Melissa in front of her steel '32 Model B outside her home in Doncaster, UK.

This Page and Opposite Page: Details of Melissa's striping on her husband's '32 pickup truck.

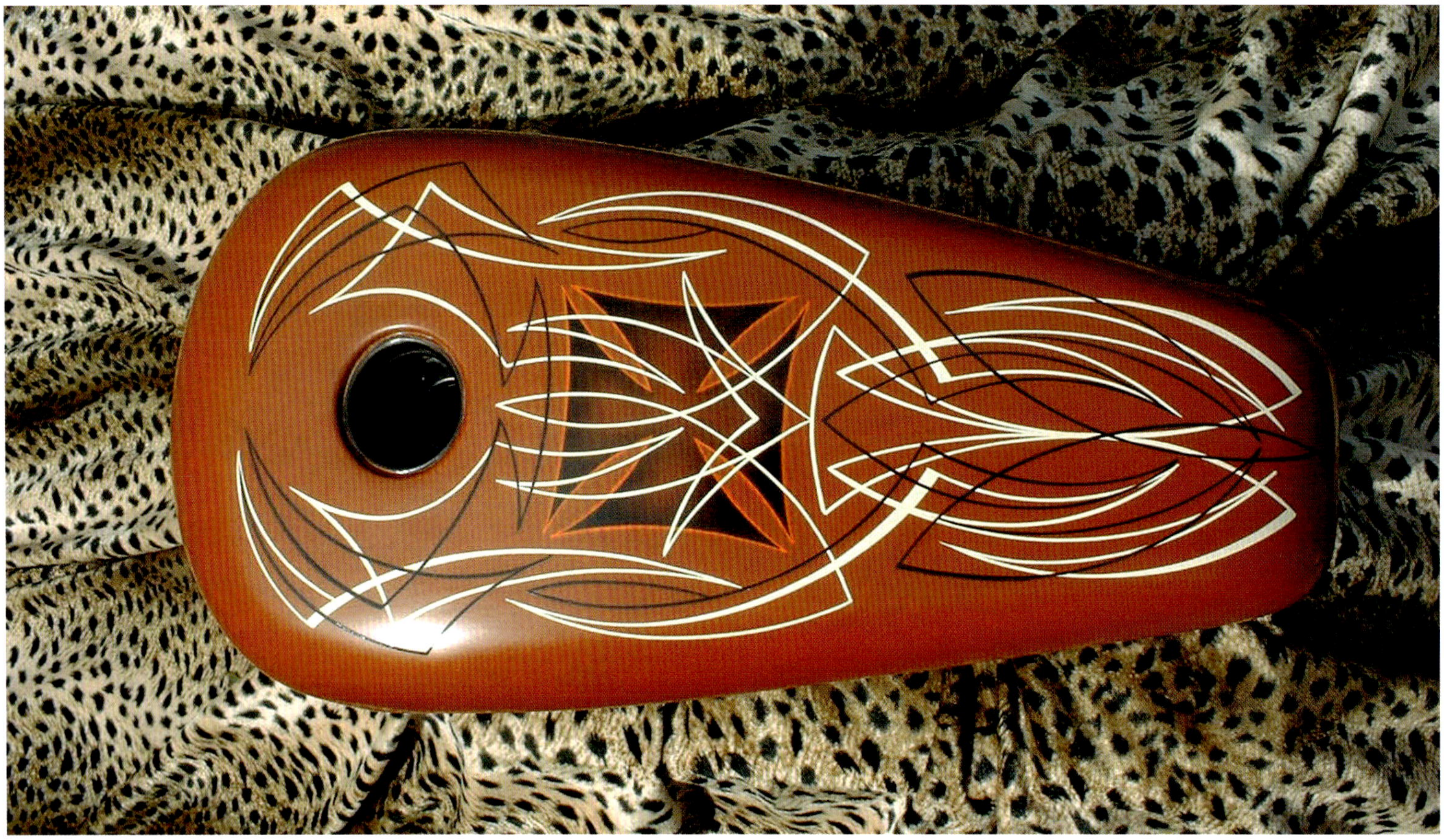

Opposite Page:
Top: Bike gas tank striped with iron cross motif.
Bottom: 1932 grille with flying eyeball motif.

This Page: Panel Art, 2006.

Neil Melliard

"South London, where I grew up, had a great Kustom scene – the Chelsea Cruise in the '70s and early '80s was massive."

"Down the road from me was American Autoparts, with great Cal Custom stuff in the window and three Superbirds parked outside... It was there when I was 14 that I bought my first airbrush with a copy of Petersen's *Creative Customizing*. That was my first foray into paint."

By age 19 Neil was on a greyhound bus on his way to the '84 Street Nats in Columbus, Ohio, and continued on to California and the Carlsbad Drag Strip. Back in London, he signed up for a signwriting course, met his future wife Mandy (also a signwriter), and started hanging out with a bunch of Aussies and Kiwis. So the next big trip was to Aus: "The Antipodeans were without exception, highly skilled, fast as hell, and great company." A few months at Alhouse and Geiger's sign shop in Sidney were followed by a tour of the East Coast in a Toyota panel van.

Back home, Neil quickly established himself as one of the top stripers in the U.K. His clients range from an F1 team to the Pro Mods drag cars of Malcolm Francis, and the Super Gas cars of Tim Adam. Neil also stripes at the major U.K. and Europe bike and car shows (including Xtreme Wheels in London and the VolksWorld Show). The influences come from Art Schilling, Steve Brown (much missed), Terry Bull, Jon Leeson, Jimmy C, and Pekka Mannemann.

Neil is optimistic about the future: "The state of striping in Britain has never been better – lots of new stripers are emerging from the VW nostalgia scene. There's a groundswell of young talent."

Opposite Page: Right: 18 and 22k gold leaf, with matte highlights, airbrushed and striped. All on reverse of glass.
Left: Kafka inspired panel.

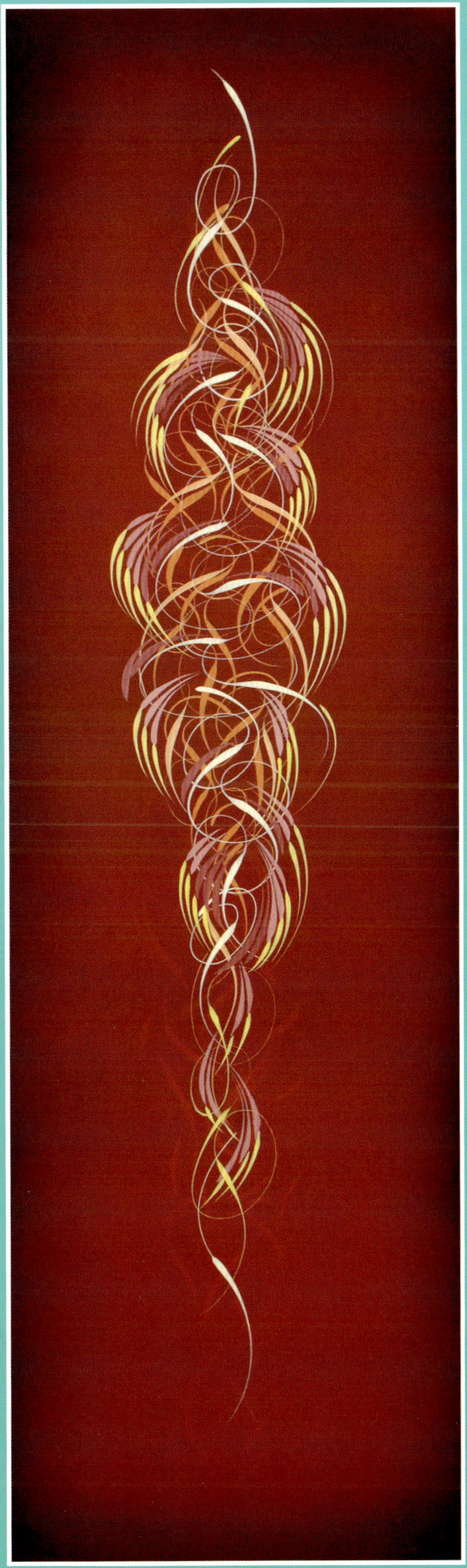

Melliard's
PINSTRIPING
SERVICE
Restorations
Customs
Race Cars
STIRLING
Letterheads
1998

This Page: Traditional pinstriping on '32 roadster.

Top Left: Striping demo at *VolksWorld* Show '06.
Top Right: Rear glass on the Prosign bus with abalone shell insert.
Bottom Left: Jim Turnbull's blown flathead '32. Trad striping over red candy.
Bottom Right: "The Sting" – an ex-Texas-based VW-powered Fiat Spyder gasser. Imported to England and restored by The Paintbox. Gold flake base with Melliard-applied red candy and variegated gold lettering.

This Page: "The Delinquent", a bobbed and hopped-up period Kustom1951 Triumph Speed Twin, built by The Baron's Speed Shop. Small blue flake layed on by The Baron, striping and lettering by Neil Melliard of Prosign, London, England. Photography by Paul Bryant , Paul Roach and Steve Hole. Model: Von Beatnik.

"The Zombie," chopped 1965 Triumph Bonneville, hopped-up, and built by The Baron's Speed Shop. Striping and lettering by Neil Melliard. Photography by Paul Roach and Steve Hole.

Pekka Wizzz

"The 1997 Arctic Pinheads moment was brilliant – under this banner we have some 30 stripers in Finland now."

Right: Pekka by his stand at the Arctic Pinheads meeting, 2005.
Background: "Rat Finn."

Opposite Page: "Lady Luck" poster design.

Pekka Mannermaa, a.k.a. Pekka Wizzz, is arguably the most influential pinstriper in Scandinavia and the key mover behind Stripe-O-Rama in 1997, which resulted in the foundation of the Arctic Pinheads. Many of the Pinheads' younger members have since got their spark from Pekka's work.

Pekka can recall his first encounter with striping precisely: the Stockholm Hot Rod Show of 1974, where he saw Ingemar Becker laying stripes on a bucket-T. Exploring the genre, he discovered the work of his major early influences – Big Daddy Roth, Robert Williams and his "Devil with a Torch" painting, European cartoonists Ever Meulen and Philip Castle, and the ubiquitous Von Dutch.

Pekka has a small workshop in Turku, near Helsinki, but also shows on the road – at A-Bombers in Sweden and at Arctic Pinhead gatherings "painting in the darkest night outdoors with only a small torch for light." His great respect for the modern masters around the world shines through – Ed Newton "one of the greatest custom car artists of all time;" Hajime Sorayama's "outstanding pin-ups;" Coop's "unbelievable use of pen," and Alan Johnson's "great attitude for young stripers." It's a great time time to be a part of Kustom Kulture he says, with more cool cars and great craftsmen than ever. Pekka also points to a trend of street-art influences getting stronger and artists being more into merging styles, a departure from the 1970s, when vans, muscle cars, drag cars and tiki rarely mixed.

He is also wary of the fads – "the tv-shows and the other retail rip-off stuff" but he is convinced that the quality work – minimalist as well as elaborate – will stand the test of time.

LADY LUCK
ZZZ
Hot Rod
Equip.

Old Cool

Wheels
HOT ROD

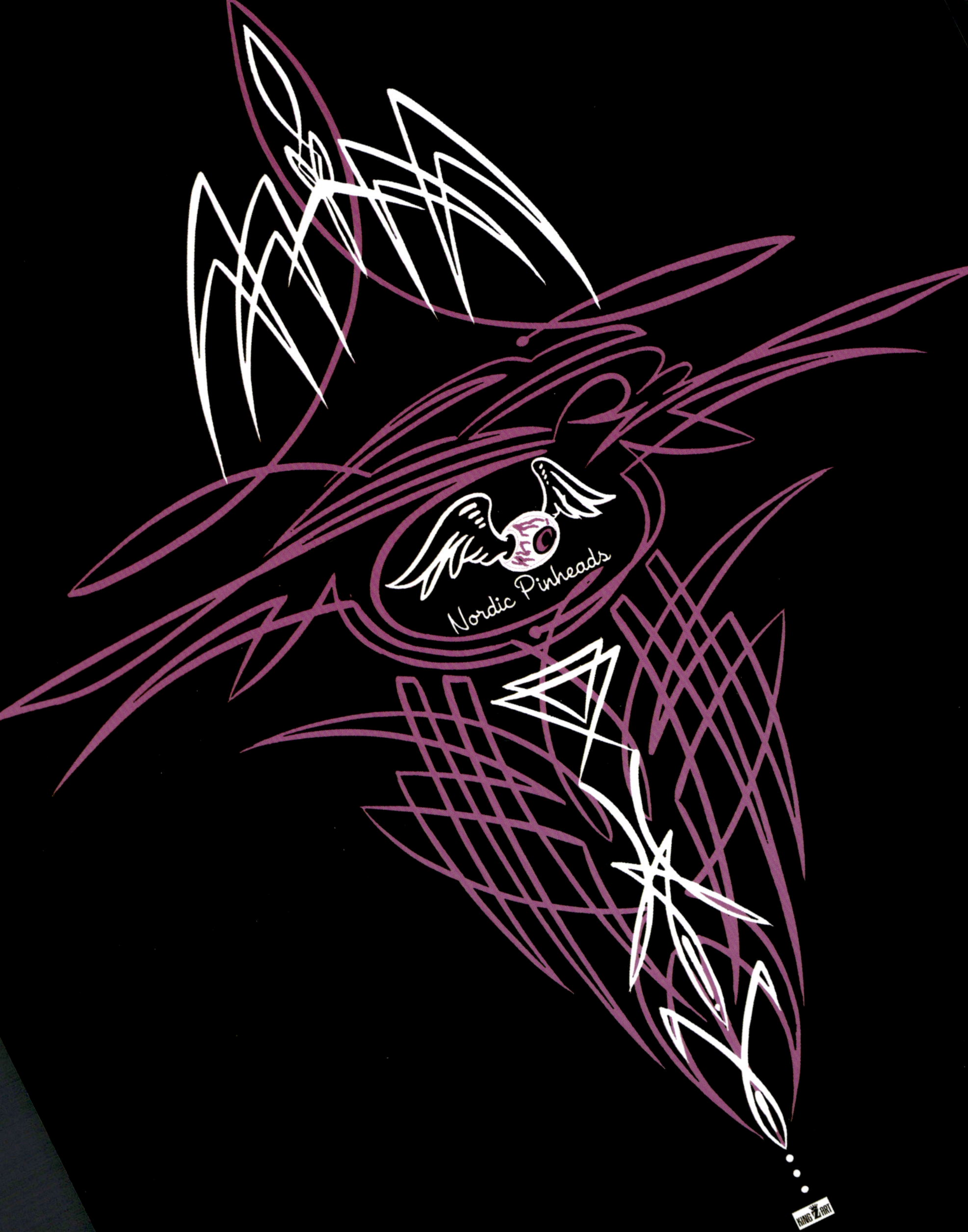
Nordic Pinheads
KING Z ART

Above: Panel Art, "Jammin' the Scandinavian Way."
Left: Panel Art, "Monster Car."

Opposite Page: T-shirt design for Nordic Pinheads.

Previous Pages:
Left: "Old Cool" T-shirt design.
Right: "Hot Rod Wheels" T-shirt design.

WHEELS
CLASSIC

Opposite Page: "Classic Wheels" T-shirt design.

This Page:
Top: Pekka's Pontiac ride with scallops and striping.
Bottom: "Stripeomon" striped metal tray with dagger-brush monster motif.
Background: "Rat Finn."

Sven von Lynch

"Going to meets, seeing other people's styles and techniques: that's the best inspiration for an artist."

Above: Sven off to work in his paintshop with cars stripped and primed, ready for their first coat. Sven carries his signature "I C Lines" case.

Opposite Page:
Top: Striped retro red phone in Sven's appartment.
Bottom: Striped helmet for Mary Ellen.

Sven discovered striping while living for a short time in Minnesota, USA, but not at a car show or in a paintshop: "In Minneapolis there was a place called Bob's Java Hut, and they had the walls covered in pinstriping. Even the tiny coffee cups were striped." The friend who took him there was Jim Schaefer's son (Schaefer was a renowned Hot Rod builder who created the famed "Stage Fright" car) and in 2000 he gave Sven some brushes and paints for his birthday. That got him started.

The early influences were the Minnesota stripers Dave Bell, Dave Ekel, Dan Picasso and Dick Bird. As Sven got into it, he got additional inspiration from Old Skool founders Dean Jeffries, Von Dutch and Monte "The Sticker Guy." More recently, "The Scandinavian King of pinstriping, Pekka Wizzz, has impacted my work."

Now based in Stockholm, Sweden, Sven works mostly alone but shares "common ideals and similarities of style with my peers from La Pantura Art Show." He also stripes at the Arctic Pinheads meets and at Stripe-O-Rama in Finland. "I still think the best show was the La Pantura group show of 2002 at Daniel Soderlund's studio."

Sven's work ranges from auto work to sign painting. He likes the influence that striping has beyond its core adherents: "I think my most influential work is probably the stuff used by creatives in advertising for inspiration." He also enjoys showing at bars and cafes in addition to auto shows. His best work: "Well, maybe the May Day Cafe sign, where I got to work with Forrest Wozniak and Phil Vandervaart (the latter is big in the movie business)." Sven sees a great future for striping: "You'll find it soon on military vehicles, and even androids."

Mary-Ellen

RATHER
LAUGH WITH THE
Sinners

BATES

This Page and Opposite Page: "Saints and Sinners" bike built by Robin Jönsson, striped by Sven and photographed by Jakob Bergström.

ELECTROLUX

vonSven's

Opposite Page:
Top Left: "Mickey" whisky flask with skull and crossbones.
Center Left: Purse with flying eyeball.
Top Right: Striped Original DePalma fridge.
Bottom: Striped detailing from trunk of car.

This Page: Striped bowling pin on box, with Nordic monster motif.

MMX 996

The Bully
POY 083

Opposite Page:
Top: Buick Eight with striped hood in Sven's workshop. **Bottom:** "The Bully."

This Page: Barber's chair, with "Missy's" striped bag.

Top: Buick with striped hood.
Below Left: Von Sven's sign with motto.
Below Right: Striped skateboards.

Opposite Page: Striped leather jacket.

Grytan
Custom

Tom Plate

"I guess I was the first 'freestyle' pinstriper to appear at a German car show; in those days Old-Skool Kustom Kulture was practically unknown in Germany."

Seven years ago Tom Plate, then training to be an illustrator, came across the book *Kustom Kulture* in Crypt Records in Hamburg and discovered Von Dutch. That same week, he read an article on how to stripe in a vintage car magazine and decided to get all the stuff. He never looked back.

"It was hard to find any info on striping in Germany or to see it in action; the car shows consisted mostly of restored Originals, hopped-up Camaros, pimpy Corvettes and pink Cadillacs. You couldn't even get 1 Shot paints; I had to use Humbrol." Everything changed when Tom decided to launch his Pinstriping Extravaganza in 2004, to which a bunch of Finns came, including Wizzzard, Platu, and Tin and Jussi Alasalmi. Suddenly, there was a lot of press interest and the show also spawned a bevvy of younger stripers. It also fixed Tom as a fixture on the European scene, where he has shown at Bedrock in Denmark, Roadrunner's paradise in Finowfurt, and Stripe-O-Rama in Finland – where in 2006 he did "my best live work."

Von Dutch was obviously the first and strongest influence, but Tom says he learns something new from everyone he meets. He also seeks inspiration from other sources, "Even those 1950s bamboo-leaf slash motifs you see on regular household items."

He sees the art growing – "Maybe one day to mobile phones and house facades" – but is typically modest about his influence, although he is proud of having designed a new brush, the Gladius. Tom works alone, but also loves a good get-together. "I love the striping world – it's a case of let's stripe and see where it gets us!"

Left: Tom striping a '32 grille at a show in Germany.
Top: Tom striping the dash of a yellow hot rod.
Bottom: "Bug."

Left and Above: Silkscreen poster for "The Great European Pinstriping Extravaganza!" in Hamburg, 2005.

Top Left: Purple striped objects: bowling pin, skull and tin box.
Top Right: "Savage Hipsters" life preserver.
Bottom: "Cheryl the Chainsaw." Customized 1967 Dolmar saw with stripes, flames and wing mirror, 2004.
Opposite Page: Tiki T-shirt design.

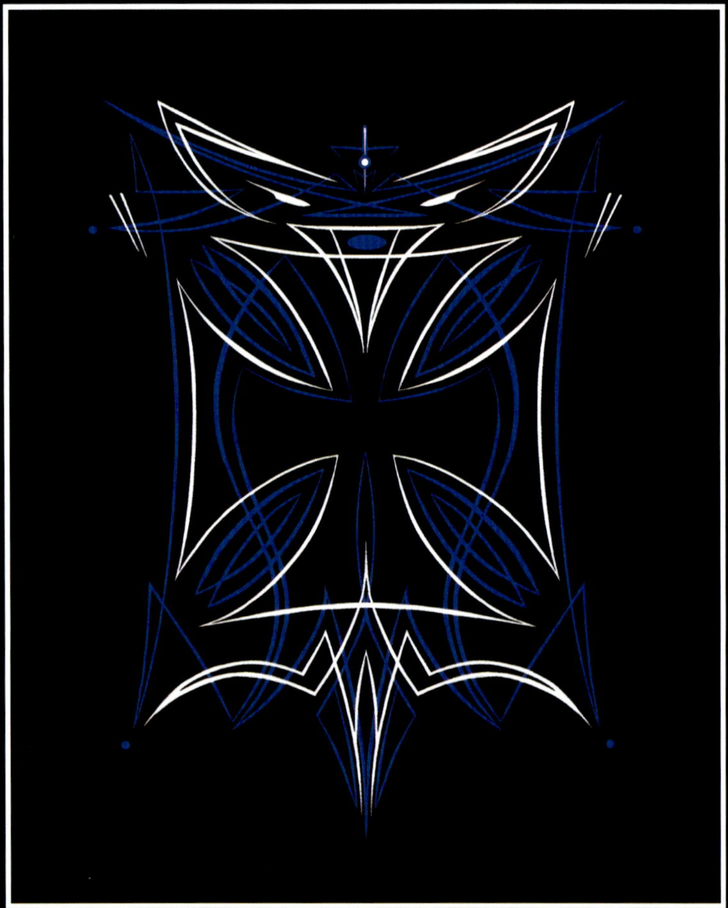

This Page: Tom T-shirt designs.

Opposite Page: T-shirt design with Pickelhaube (spiked German helmet) and skull motifs.

This Page: Tom: "This one was done at a small festival in Sønderborg, on a flat red Impala. The owner wanted something simple yet stylish, with an Iron Cross motif... The hard part was making the two motifs on the upper and the rear part of the trunk lid into one, over the crease... Nah, it wasn´t that hard."

This Page: Tom: "I was really hot for striping this car. When was the last time you had the chance to stripe a Kaiser Dragon? It belongs to some crazy Finns, who panscraped that beast all over Europe, still with the original flat-six... I tried to make the pinstriping look like it had been on for ages, so I mixed an off-white, sometimes adding a little more matte brown, for that faded look, and finished it with sand before it was completely dry... Mission accomplished."

JAPAN & AUSTRALIA

Ranchero GT

Opposite Page : Striped Ford Ranchero, with lace-spray detailing on sides.

Right: Enamel.

Enamel

"I made my US debut at the 1998 Rat Fink Reunion in Santa Fe Springs, CA - and I keep going back for inspiration. There is such a great vibe in California, and it keeps getting better."

One of the new group of pinstripers who followed Hiro "Wildman" Ishii's pioneering work in Japan, Enamel was also inspired early on by the work of Ed "Big Daddy" Roth.

Born in 1966 in Iwaki City, Fukushima, Japan, Enamel stayed put and began pinstriping in 1990 from a small studio in Iwaki. He is passionate about achieving the right metallic look and uses 1 Shot sign enamel or House of Kolor urethane enamel for his designs.

"I guess about 20% of my work takes place in the studio and the rest is special commissions, for which I travel all over Japan."

The US influence is clear and Enamel has spent a lot of time at the key shows – the Rat Fink Reunions as well as the Cruisin' Nationals at Paso Robles, CA.

Enamel remains passionate about his cars. "I am crazy about all the hot rod cars, but most of all I lavish time on my 1959 Chevrolet El Camino."

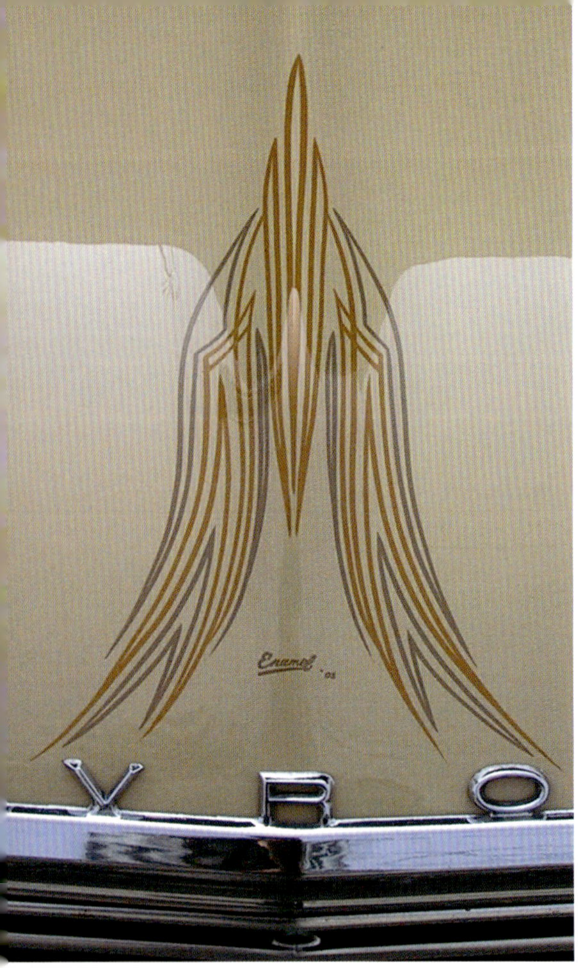
Enamel

Chevrolet
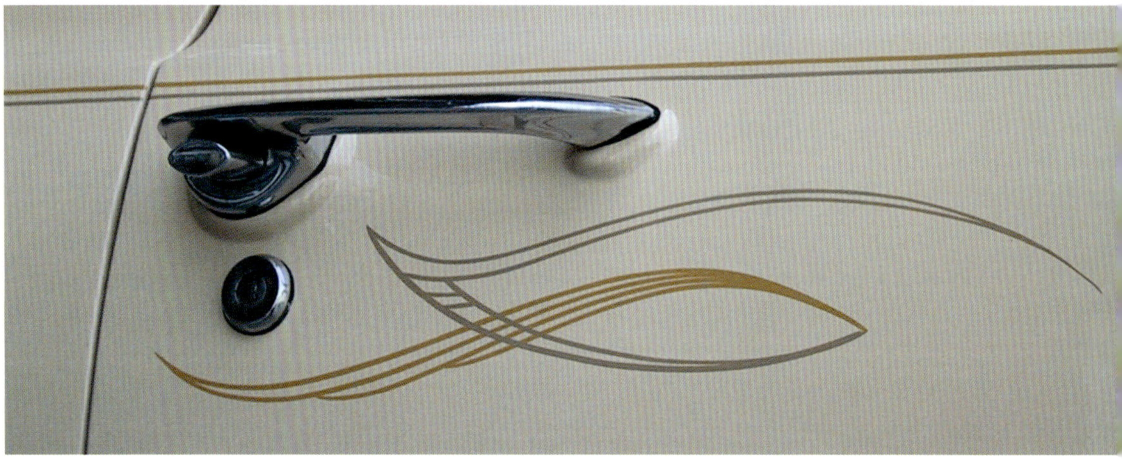

Opposite Page: Striping and stripe details on a 1960s Chevy II.

This Page: Striping on "Rebellion" bike.

Right: Striped "Fireman" panel.
Far Right: Wildman striping a new Mini Cooper.

Opposite Page: Poster for 2005 Mooneyes Christmas Party in Yokohama.

MOONEYES
X'mas Party
2005
CAR SHOW
LIVE BANDS
ARTISTS
VENDORS
Saturday Dec. 10th. '05
at the
"STAR ACADEMY"
Custom Culture
Information: MOONEYES™
562-944-6311 www.mooneyes.com
Car Show
Pre '64 Cars only!
Rat Fink™ © Roth '86

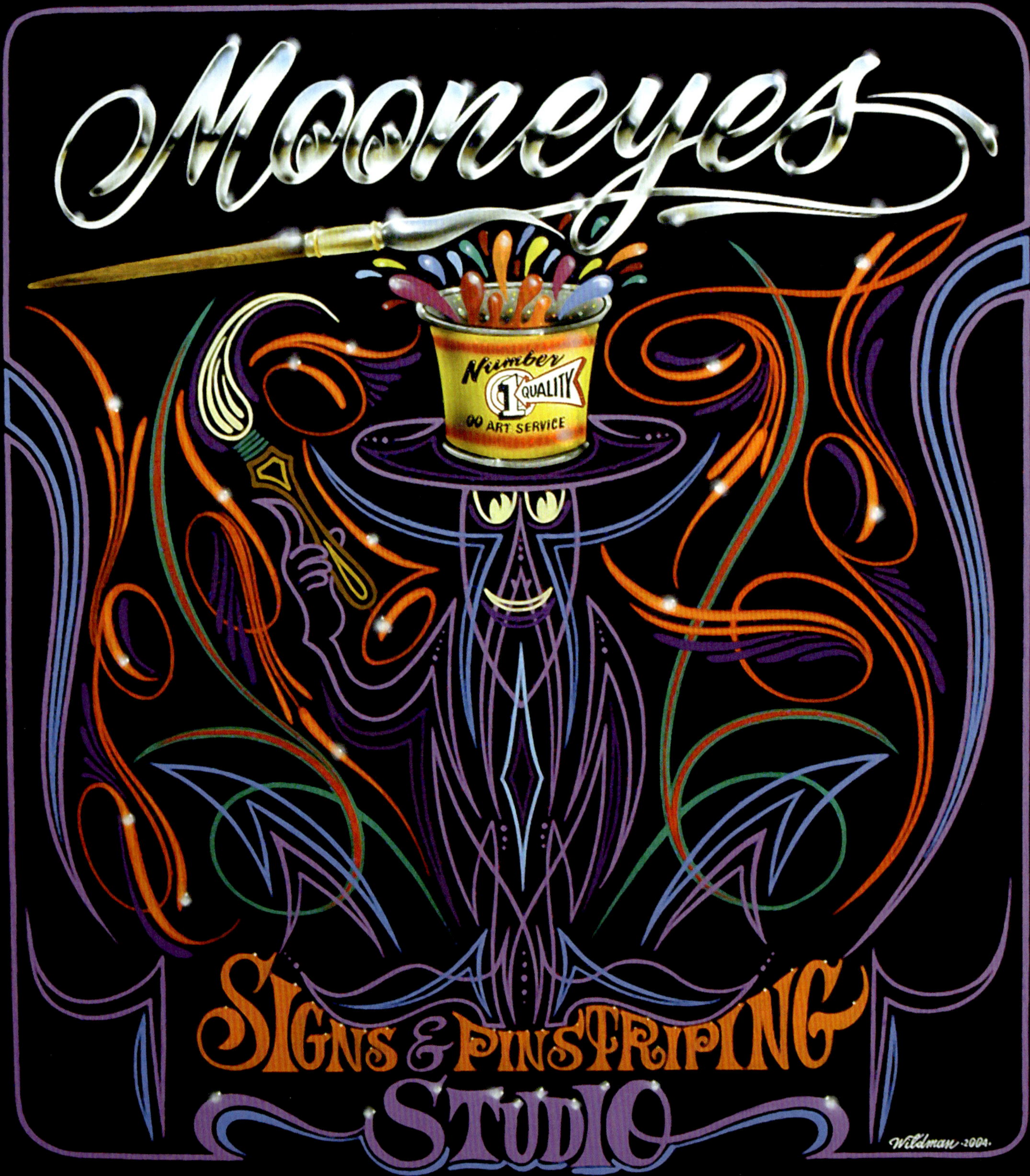
Mooneyes
Number 1 QUALITY
OO ART SERVICE
SIGNS & PINSTRIPING
STUDIO
Wildman 2004.

Right: Poster design for Crown Classics Picnic, 2002.

Opposite Page: Panel for Mooneyes Studio.

Above: Panel art for Mooneyes studio.

Page Opposite: Rat Fink Reunion T-shirt design, 2005.

Rat Fink Reunion
2005
MAZOOMA!
AUG. 6, 2005
HOSTED BY
MOONEYES
SWEDEN

Ken the Flattop

"In the process of drawing a line, I feel so great when it turns out to be the one I exactly want. The reason I keep pinstriping is to get that great feeling."

Top: Photo of Flattop by DEE Inagaki.
Page Opposite: "Peace (three monkeys)" poster design.

Born in Yokohama, in 1969, Ken the Flattop is one of the most versatile stripers in Japan today. As a kid Ken was obsessed with cars: "Drawing cars was my favorite thing to do. Since then, nothing has changed. I still enjoy it more than anything." By the time he was a teenager, this interest turned into a fascination with the whole American hot rod scene, and Ken never looked back.

Out of his studio in Yokohama, Ken today churns out an impressive body of work, from striping cars and motorbikes, to sign painting in general, T-shirt design, magazine illustration work, posters and, perhaps his favorite, surfboards. Ken's close connection with the Japanese surfing scene is an extension of his fascination with California. His striping on boards is celebrated in Japan, and he is a regular at the Flashbugs meetings, on Oiso Long Beach, which sees the biggest annual gathering of bugs and Karmann Ghias. His surfing designs also reveal a strong Tiki influence.

Ken is spreading his art through clever merchandising. He collaborates closely with the Bo Sports, Mahal and Un Gran Sol businesses; with the latter he was the lead artist in their *Alta Muchacha* exhibition. His regular blog brings punters into his website, where more merchandise is available.

When does he relax? "On Sundays. Sunday is BBQ day on the beach."

Peace
KEN THE FLATTOP PAINT SERVICE

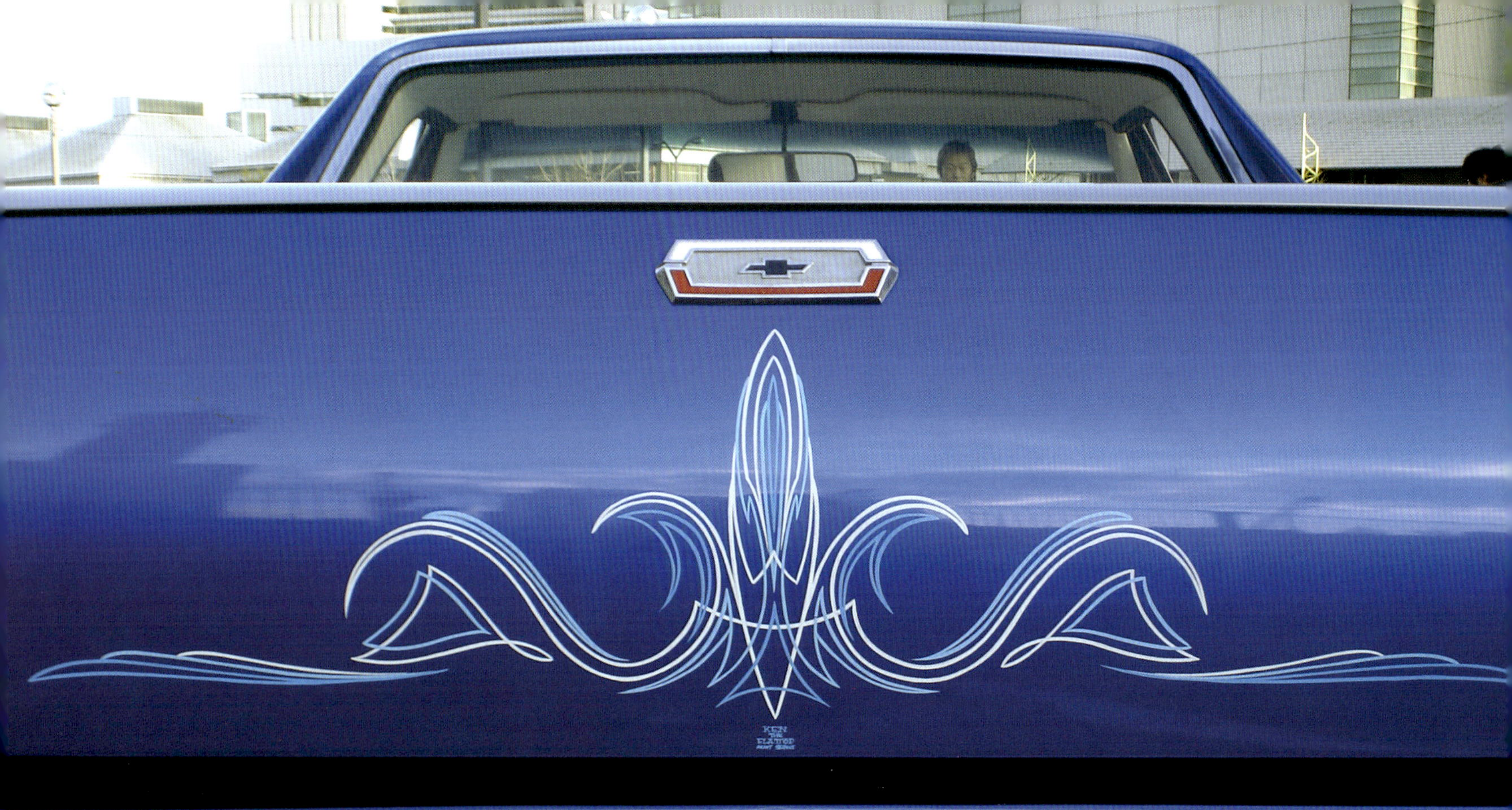

This Page: Drop-flap and hood stripe detailing on a '69 El Camino.

Page Opposite:
Top: Helmet design of Japanese evil character "ONI".
Middle: Striped 'Mexican Skull' helmet image.
Bottom: Striped butterfly on an '86 El Camino.

KFT
MONSTER
RIDE

GT
the GEISYA
KILLER
SAPPORO
KUSHIRO
SENDAI
HAKATA
OKAYAMA
KYOTO
MIYAZAKI
KOHCHI
OHSAKA
YOKOHAMA
YAIZU
YOKOSUKA
NAGU

The Original
COYOTE COUNTY
CRUISERS
by
KEN THE FLATTOP
PAINT SERVICE

Top Left: Birthday card design.
Left: Card design.
Top Right: Namecard.

Page Opposite:
Far Left: Snowboard with original character design – and pinstripes – on candy green paint.
Left: T-shirt designs "GT the Geisya Killer" and "Coyote Country Cruisers", 1 Shot paint on aluminium board.

Below: Makoto in his garage.
Right: Striping on a signature Makoto Fortune Cat.

Opposite Page: Poster "Hot Rod to Hell" design for *Juxtapoz* magazine.

Makoto

"My career took off when I decided to paint a Fortune Cat – I now keep it permanently in my studio for good luck. I think it's probably working."

Born in Aichi, Japan in 1968, Makoto Kobayashi loved cars as far back as he can remember and bought his first, a 1972 VW, at the age of 18.

With his VW he attended many of the Mooneyes car shows and it was at one of these that he met Hiro "Wildman" Ishii and first saw a pinstripe demo. By 1996 Makoto had set up his own pinstriping studio and his skills developed fast.

Attending a Spring Burst show in Japan he met the artist who had most influenced him – California's Jimmy C. From then on he started showing in the US as well as Japan, attending Mooneyes Rat Fink Reunion in 2000 before presenting his first solo show in the States, entitled "Made in Japan" at the Cacao Coffee House in Santa Monica. The show was sponsored by *Burnout* magazine and led in turn to Makoto being the only Japanese artist to take part in the *Von Dutch: an American Original* show in Northridge.

His first solo show in Japan, *Kustom City*, followed in 2003 and was a huge succes.

Makoto's signature Fortune Cat certainly worked. A Makoto original is today highly prized and the show credits speak for themselves. There are too many to list here, but recent ones include: The Ed "Big Daddy" Roth Group exhibition, L.A.; *Cut 'n Drive*, Burbank; *Juxtapoz* 10th Anniversary Party, San Francisco, and *Try Power* in Pasadena.

JUXTAPOZ

This Page: Selection of T-shirt and panel art, including (Top Right) Hanya Poster with metallic gold paint on matte black.

Opposite Page: Top Left: "Magic of Pinstriping" poster. **Top Right:** Rat Fink panel. **Bottom Left:** Tattoo-inspired "Domestic/Exotic" poster. **Bottom Right:** Tattoo-inspired Lady Luck, with 8-ball bikini, horseshoe hair, and four aces.

Magic of Pinstriping
KUSTOM KULTURE

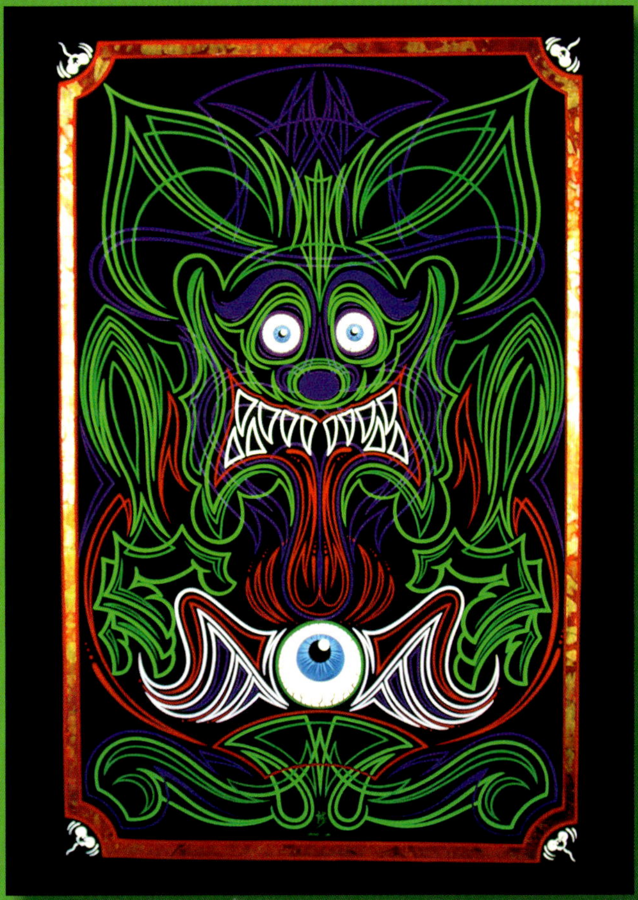

GREASER
KUSTOM
KULTURE
DOMESTIC

M&K
CUSTOM SIGNS.COM
GLD 204

MAGIC OF PINSTRIPING
&
KUSTOM KULTURE
M&K
CUSTOM
SIGNS
6-15-8 Ueji Okazaki
Aichi 444-0823 Japan
Tel: 0564-54-1911
WWW.MANDKCUSTOMSIGNS.COM

M&K
CUSTOM SIGNS.COM
THX 138

2005
SUN APRIL 10
AM10:00 START!!
CAR SHOW & LIVE
LINX-PARKING
MIYAZAKI BEACH, KIRA
INFORMATION
The Candies CAR CLUB
090.4156.6030

This Page: Striped paintings on canvas.

Opposite Page:
Top and Bottom Left: Striped paintings on canvas.
Top Right: Poster for Makoto's shop.
Bottom Right: Poster for Candies Car Club show on Miyazaki Beach, 2005.

GOLD DIGGER
CENTURY
MODESTO
TOPPERS

W. SHIZUOKA

GARAGE

Wet Dream

This Page:
Top Left and Right: Makoto posters for Candies Car Club shows.
Left: Poster for Makoto's shop in Aichi, Japan.
Above: Poster for *Kustom City II* art show at Face Pop Gallery.

Opposite Page: Makoto paintings on canvas.

Minoru "Mr. G" Goto

" I always incorporate a Tiki motif in my work, whether it's pinstriping or painting."

Above: Mr G with a Tiki mug.

Opposite Page:
Left: Two posters for *California Screamin'* Hot Rod and Art Show.
Right: Artwork of Tiki God, sitting on piston head with striping brush.

One of the rare left-handed pinstripers, Minoru came across pinstriping through Wildman's pinstriping demonstration in 1992. From then on he was hooked and combined his status as the Tiki pioneer in Japan with his pinstriping art.

Like many in the Japanese scene, he established close links with pinstripers in the US early on. This culminated in his first one-man show in L.A. in 2005, where all the works on offer sold out.

Tiki is an obsession of Mr G's. He is one of the foremost collectors of Tiki mugs in Japan and recently created an original Tiki mug design for the leading Tiki manufacturers, Tiki Farm, of San Clemente, CA.

Mr G's studio is now in Fukuoka Prefecture and his studio to outside commission work is roughly 50/50. He likes advertising some personal details: "My blood type is O, my favourite food is rice omelette, I drive a 1952 Ford and I also want you to quote my motto: You Gotta Run When You Gotta Run." We're not sure quite sure what he means there, but the artistry speaks for itself.

CALIFORNIA
SCREAMIN'
Gasoline
PRESENTS

CALIFORNIA
SCREAMIN'
Gasoline
PRESENTS

KUSTOM KULTURE

Above: "Starlite" T-shirt design.

Opposite Page: "Exotiki" Original Island poster design.

EXOTIKI

T's Design Shop

"My real name? No name!"

Above: T laying down the line on a bike.

Opposite Page: Skull design on helmet.

T likes to retain his mystery, letting the work speak for itself.

He started his career in 1982, working for a company drawing signs. Then in 1989 he attended the 3rd Mooneyes Street Car Nationals in Japan and saw pinstriping in action for the first time. He went independent in 1990, opening T's Design Shop. The first commissions were signage for commercial vehicles. He started pinstriping for friends; by 1994 it became a serious part of the business.

Commissions flowed in, including stuff from his local hot rod shop and the local Harley Davidson dealership. In addition to attending all the major pinstriping events in Japan (most recently, with Mr G and Wildman Ishii, the 14th Annual Hot Rod and Custom show in Yokohama), T holds regular demonstrations in front of his shop: "I want to spread enthusiasm for pinstriping to a younger audience, to have the same impact that I felt when I first saw a demo in 1989," he says.

KIRIN

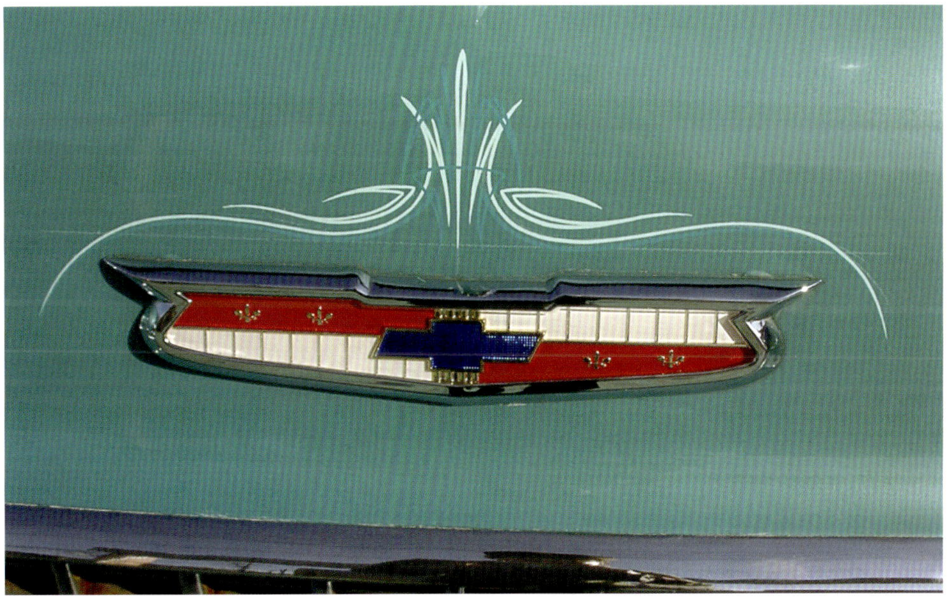

Left: T hard at work in his workshop.
Right: Examples of T's striping and lettering.

This Page: T putting the finishing touches to some flames.

Painters

Ben Lander

"The Lander agenda is to hit the road, brush in hand, see the world, then stripe it."

Opposite Page:
Top: "Vanpire" custom van, built by Cale Hummerston, with white pinstripes over its "retina-detaching" flake job.
Middle and Bottom: Ben Lander's "li'l working wagon," soon to feature no gaps at all.

In his late teens, Ben Lander fashioned a striping brush by cutting down a regular painter's brush. This led to an instant obsession: "No surface would ever feel safe again. Everything, including the furniture, became rapidly adorned in strange and wonderful symmetrical designs."

Now aged 29 and based in Perth, western Australia, Ben Lander has turned his passion for art, and all things old and automotive, into a small but growing business of striping and lettering cars and bikes from the back of a little matte black, and heavily pinstriped, wagon.

Ben doesn't acknowledge too many influences. "I like to do lots of different stuff from my Lander Studios. All sorts of weird and wonderful things spring forth from there, including the likes of oil paintings, album covers, and poster art."

When not laying down lines, Ben Lander can be found playing drums and singing in his band, The Mcarburettors, or scouring the desolate western Australian bush for old cars to drag back to his lair to be reborn "rodded."

He doesn't feel part of any particular scene: "Out here, Lander Studios is simply unique."

W.A
VANPIRE

0415 643 075
PINSTRIPING
FREE HAND
W.A.

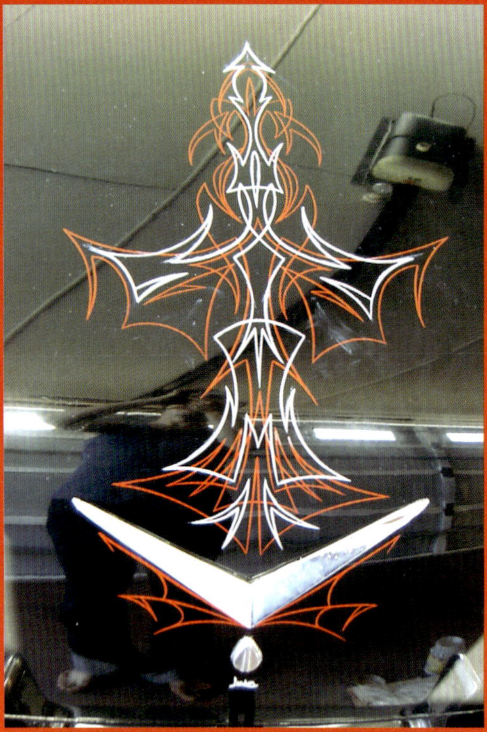

This Page: Black and red striping with web design on Ritchie Balazic's '54 Caddy Coupe deville.

Opposite Page:
Top: Ben Lander's striped business card, printed on clear acetate front and back for a 3-d effect.
Bottom Left and Middle: Chevy Silverado, with flames outlined in contemporary style, using Lander color dubbed with watermelon.
Bottom Right: "Attack of the Bubble Tops " by Lander Studios.

BEN
Lander
FREE HAND
PINSTRIPING
FLAMES/SCALLOPS
POSTER T-SHIRT
CD COVER
ART AND DESIGN
TATTOO FLASH
0415643075

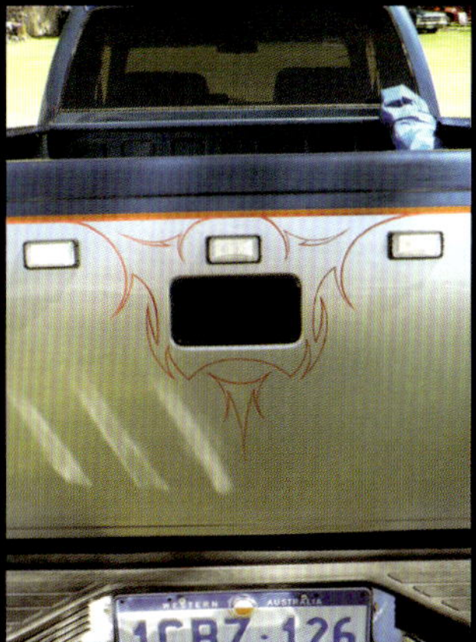

Peter Anthony

"I get paid twice for a job: the money in my pocket, and when I see the work again by thinking, "Yep – that works well."

Above: Peter signing a striped panel in his Surrey yard.

Australian Peter Anthony has been around the block. Born in Sydney, NSW, in 1952, he's also lived in Queensland, Darwin in the Northern Territories, Austria, Sri Lanka, and New Zealand before finally settling in Surrey, UK. He remembers the time he discovered pinstriping: "It was around 1970, in Coffs Harbor, NSW, Australia." The location was where Lindsey Bros. Trucking was based. Peter was struck by their Big Mack tractor units, most of which carried signwriting, stripes, and flourishes. He also remembers seeing, in a very Aussie way, striping on surfboards way back then.

He cites diverse influences, from the Czech 1900s Art Nouveau artist Alphonse Mucha, to early '70s surf culture. Closer to home it was the sign men, who numbered striping amongst their set of skills. Bruce Vandesse, New Zealander Bruce Kent, and Glenn Dick taught him a lot: "In Australia in those days it wasn't the specialty it is today. Striping was part of signage: you had to paint a wall 20 feet by 30 feet two floors up, on a swinging stage, and those stages did swing."

Peter moved to the UK in 1990 and there came into touch with a new crowd, including Neil Melliard and Terry Bull, who in turn influenced his work. While he mostly works solo, he also occasionally collaborates with Neil and Terry.

He shows regularly in the UK, and his best show remains the 1996 GoldWing owners' club in Huddersfield. The art is in a good state in Peter's view: "It's a way of life and more and more people are picking up a striping brush. I've come across florists, designers, IT lecturers, and even lawyers doing it. It's also fashionable again, with traditional panels now being used as domestic art."

His advice to newcomers? "Relax, have fun, and don't try too hard!"

Above: "Match, Fuse and Grenade" striped panel.
Left: "Summertime" panel, paint on pearl surface.

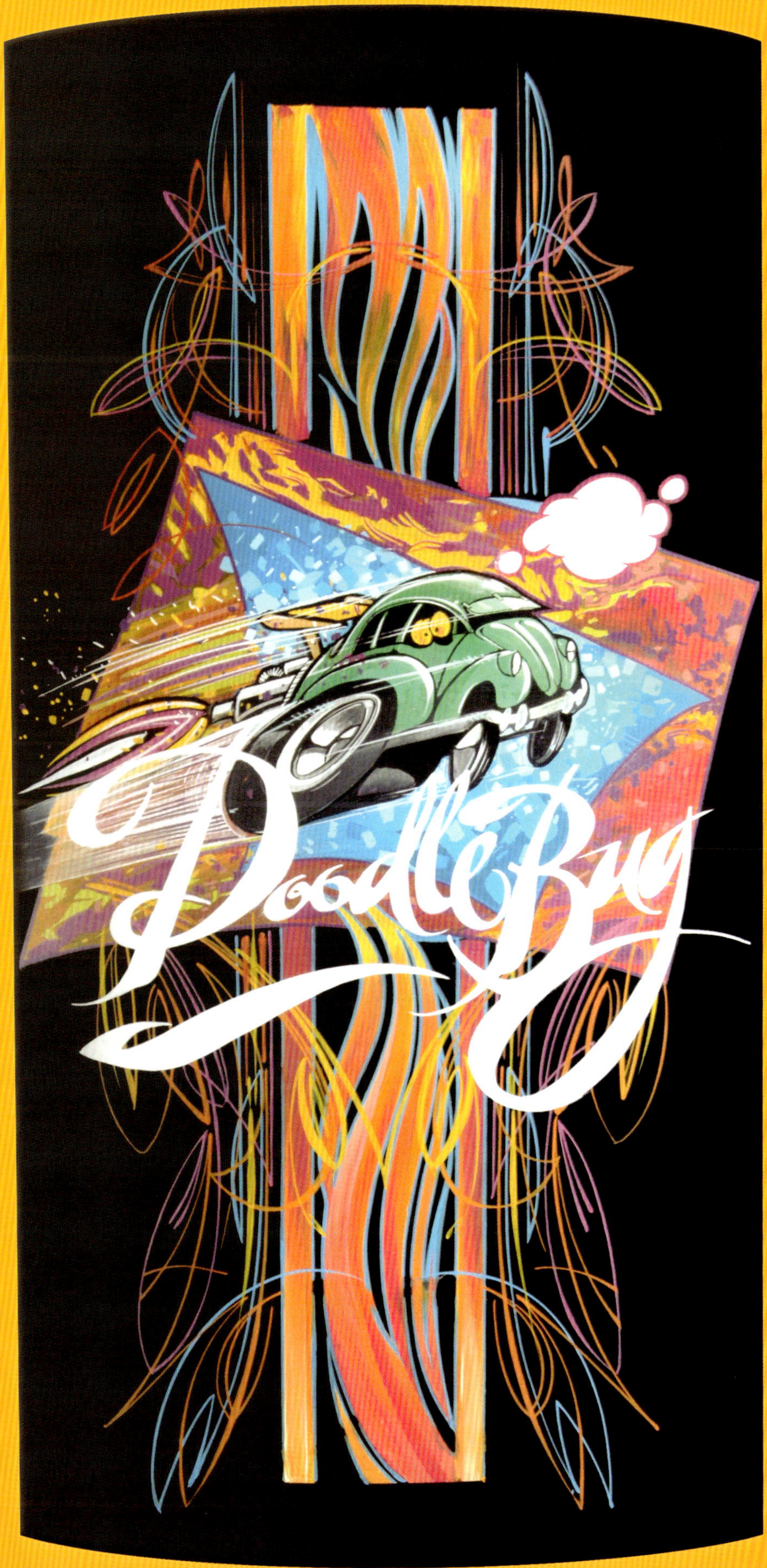

Left: "Doodle Bug" striped panel.
Above: "Hunky Dory" panel.

Opposite Page: Striped panel, designed for hanging at home.

Left: How Simon imagines himself when he races at the Nostalgia Drags.

Opposite Page: Lynn's 49 Ford incorporates a not-so-subtle flamed theme, as requested by the owner. Simon: "Lynn is a cool gal who did a lot of the work on that custom herself, squirreled away in her boyfriend's workshop in Bedfordshire, UK."

"Don's Triumph is a resurrected '70s chopper brought into the 21st century both stylewise and performance-wise, with a mad tiki monster on the tank."

Simon Watts

"I loved striping because it was the absolute opposite of my job – at the time it was my only creative outlet."

When doing Fine Art at college in Australia, Simon's ambition was to live the life of an artist. But the practical streak got the better of him and he switched to doing Graphic Design and then a job in an office, "Thinking up stupid advertising campaigns for dumb clients."

Rob Walker "creative dynamo...reminded me that cars were a creative outlet." This took Simon to get his hot rod and custom fix at Paso Robles, CA. Two life-changing things happened – he met Angie, his future wife, and he saw pinstripers at work. "The reason I was instantly attracted was that striping represented total creative freedom and a return to my first love: painting."

Simon went all-out, videoing and photographing stripers at work (remember this was the 80s, before digital) in detail. Moving to the UK, he discovered a cool scene – "The result of the Hot Rod and music scenes being so closely related" – and one which allowed you "to hang out 4 or 5 nights a week with like-minded drunkards." As his confidence with striping grew he started renting a booth at shows and doing striping demos in public.

Back in Australia, he made the switch he'd promised himself all those years back — to being a full-time artist. He now shows annually at Paso Robles, "Where everyone assumes I'm a Yank." He's also hooked up, thanks to The Pizz, with the Artists at Large collective out of Kansas, as well as showing in France, Italy, Holland, Finland, and Japan.

His individual style has emerged from a distillation of other's work – and he finds that he can "hit that groove when the creative juices start to flow." His big inspirations are Ed Roth and Von Dutch: "Like them I like bold designs and minimal colors that harmonize with the car. As a rule I don't like busy design - but Jimmy C., he's the exception!"

235

OAS 235

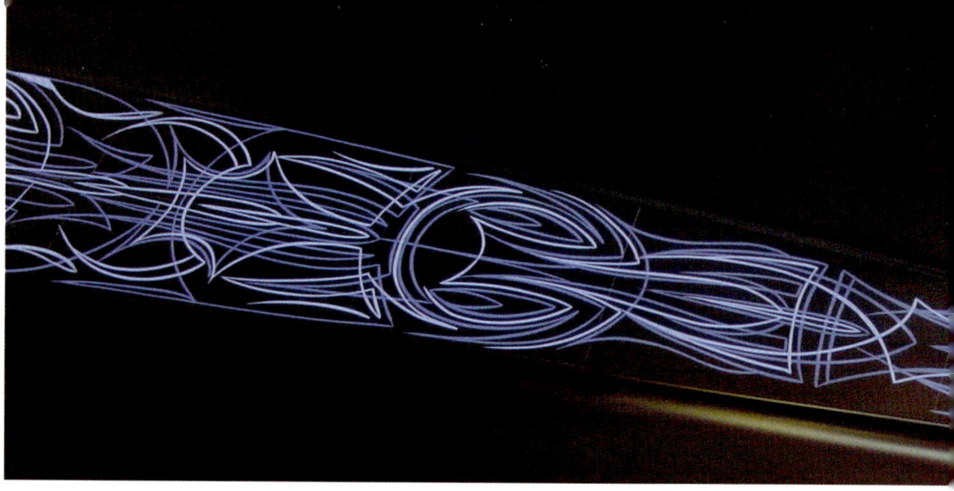

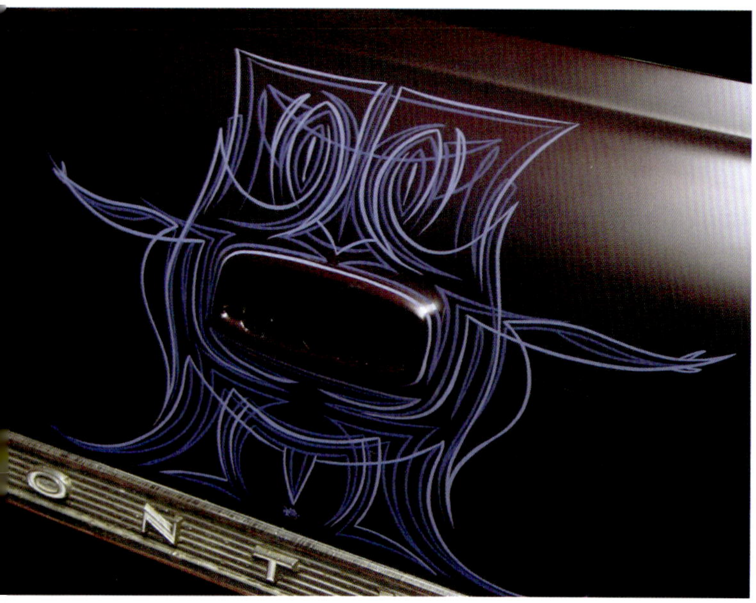

This Page: Mike's Pontiac Wagon. Simon: "Mike Scotny was a member of England's Original Low Flyers hot rod club back in the early '80s. This Pontiac wagon was his latest personal project, and got striped to within an inch of its life before final assembly."

Opposite Page:
Top: Shelley's Double Bass. Shelley is a sometime musician and full-time globe trotter. Simon: "How she keeps moving around with this piece of hand luggage I'll never know. The bass currently resides in Minnesota, USA, and wears the result of letting me go mad on it from top to bottom."

Bottom Left: Painting of Head.
Simon: "Like most stripers my background is in art. I've always painted and this is just one of my recent series of head paintings currently showing in galleries in Australia."

Bottom Right: Chris's Model A tourer from the Gold Coast of Australia.
Simon: "Three colors cover the front, back, and insides of this sweet little hauler. Chris drives the living crap out of this car, all over Australia."

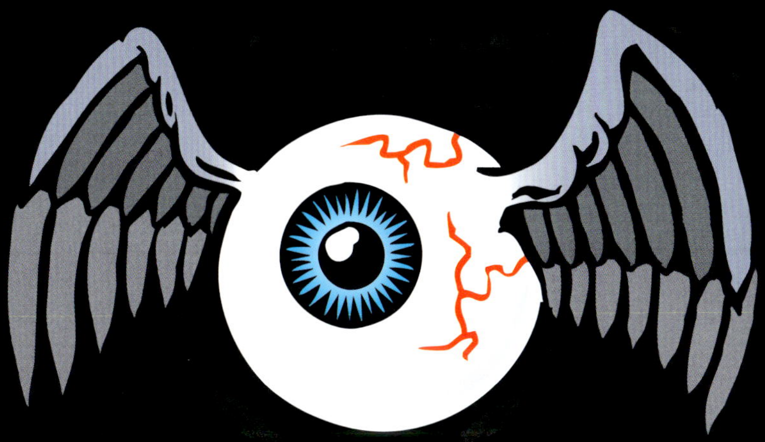

APPENDIX

ARTISTS

Website details for selected artists:

USA

Alan Johnson
Blairstown, NJ
www.alanjohnsongrafix.com

Craig Fraser
Bakersfield, CA
www.gotpaint.com

"Dirty" Donny Gillies
www.dirtydonny.com

Herb Martinez
Livermore, CA
www.herbmartinez.com

Jimmy C
San Clemente, CA
www.kustomart.com

Mr. J
Paterson, NJ
www.xcaliberart.com

Ryzart
www.ryzart.com

Skratch
Sun Valley, CA
www.kultureshoq.com

Tony Perez
Glendale, AZ
www.pinstripestony.com

Canada

Yosemite Sam
Delaware, Ontario
www.yosemitesams.com

Europe

Empire 32
Strasbourg, France
http://mapage.noos.fr/empire32

Jon Leeson
www.letterknight.co.uk

Maze
Sankt Augustin, Germany
www.mazegrafx.de

Melissa Gee
Rossington, Doncaster, England
www.lucky-stripe.com

Neil Melliard
Wallington, England
www.prosign1.co.uk

Pekka "Wizzz" Mannermaa
Turku, Helsinki, Finland
www.wiz-art.org

Tom Plate
Hamburg, Germany
www.sadsaucer.de

Von Sven
Stockholm, Sweden
www.vonsven.com

Additional artists featured in our Panel Jam pages:

Roberto Larogna
Custom Design Italy
Email: customd@hotmail.com

Peter Hammersley
North Tyneside, England
www.aurorakustomgraphics.co.uk

Kris Johnson
Leicester, England
www.pinstripinguk.com

Nefarious
Hampshire, England
www.pinstriping.co.uk

Japan

Enamel
Iwaki City, Fukushima
www.enamel-art.com

Flat Top
www.kentheflattop.com

Hiro "Wildman" Ishii
Yokohama, Kanagawa
www.mooneyes.co.jp/english/shop/studio

Makoto
Okazaki, Aichi
www.mandkcutomsigns.com

Mr. G
Fukuoka-City, Fukuoka
www.mr-gkrazyart.com

Australia

Pete Anthony
www.freestylesignstudio.co.uk

Simon Watts
Email: swattsinusa@hotmail.com

SUPPLIES

Paint and Brush Supplies

1 Shot
www.spraylat.com

House of Kolor
www.hokpaint.com

Kafka Brushes
www.kooltie.com/kafka/brushes

Mack Brushes
www.mackbrush.com

Pinstriping UK
www.pinstripinguk.com

Magazines

Auto Graphics Magazine
www.nbm.com

Auto Art Magazine
www.autoartmagazine.com

SignCraft
www.signcraft.com

Misc.

Letterhead
www.letterhead.com

Mooneyes
2-10 Honmoku Miyahara
Naka-ku, Yokohama
Japan 231-0804
Phone: 81-45-623-9600
Email: shop@mooneyes.co.jp
www.mooneyes.co.jp

CREDITS

Photos on pages 12, 14, 17, 18, 19, 20, 21, 22, 23, 24, and 25, courtesy of the **George Barris Collection.**

Color photo of Dean Jeffries, page 23, courtesy **Andy Southern, Jr.**

Photos on front cover, pages 2 and 15, courtesy **Richard Heeps**
www.richardheeps.co.uk.

Additonal Photography:
Martin Powney

Image on page 6:
"Drawing" by **Mr G**

Image on page 192:
"Self-portrait" by **Maze**

Section opener eyeballs:
Vince Ray
www.vinceray.com

Special thanks to

Neil Melliard
Roger Hawkins
John Erdos
Andrzej Michalski
Tony Thacker, Director of the NHRA Motorsports Museum
Dave at Geronimo Clothing
Simon Pollock
Paul Barrow
Sarah Amos
Serena, Isabella, and Orlanda Castello-Cortes

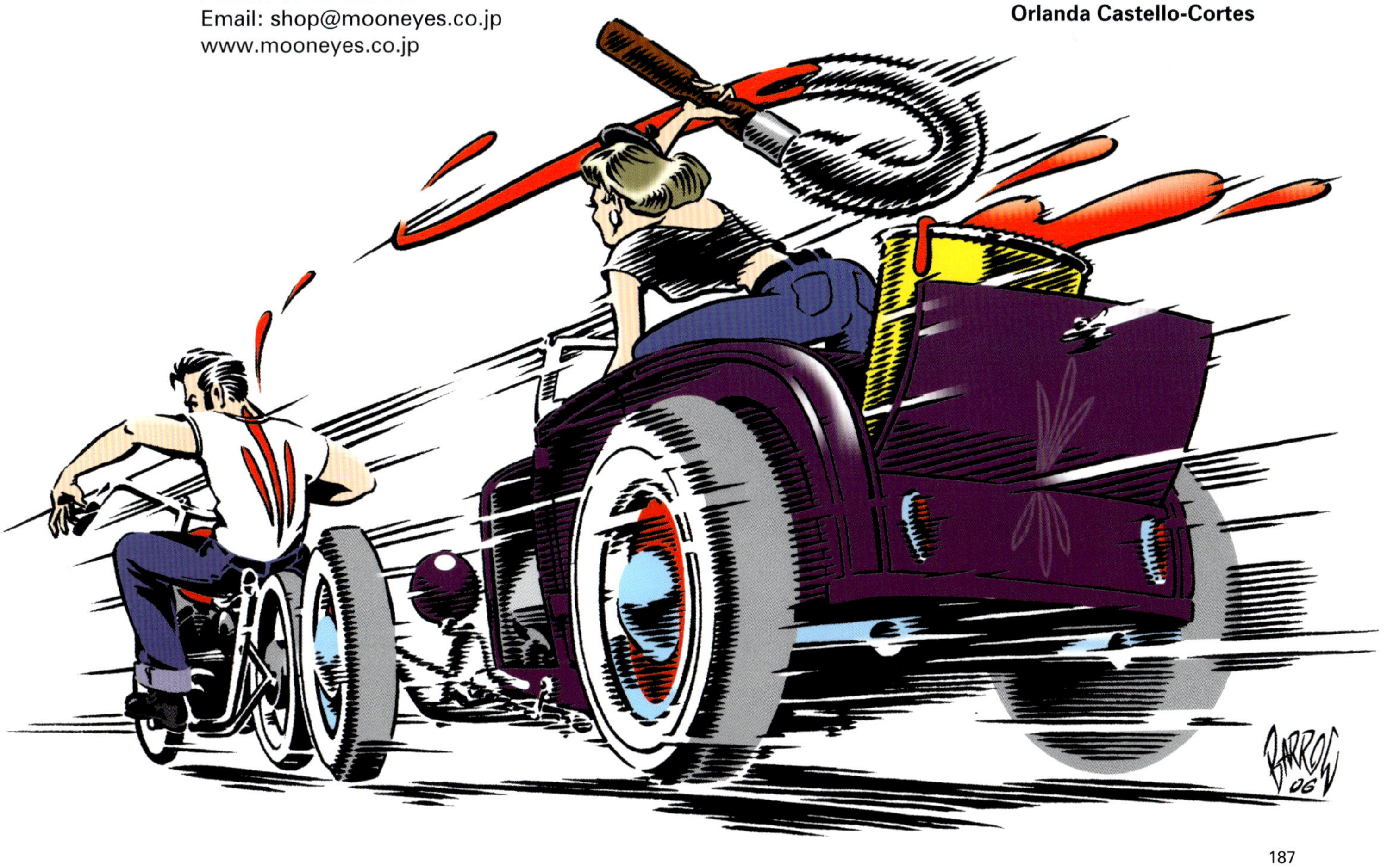

GLOSSARY

Base Color – The (usually mono color), paint surface of the vehicle on which the stripe or other design will be painted.

Bleed Through – When paint seeps under the masking tape edge, leaving a design of vertical lines starting at the edge of the painted line.

Burnishing – When working with gold leaf, the removal of excess leaf, usually with a cotton ball.

Candy Apple – Paint application (attributed to Joe Bailon) where translucent paint is layered simulating the coating on a candied apple.

Chalking – When the surface of the paint oxidizes, producing a chalky appearance.

Climb up on the Tip – Achieving a finer line from a thick brush by using the very tip of the brush (within 5% of brush length).

Coupe – A closed, two-door automobile.

Cutting In – Blocking the ends of a striped line straight by filling in.

Drag – After a few minutes on the palette, paint is a little more resistant to laying down, hence "drag."

Dry spray – When too much air pressure is used spraying paint onto a surface, resulting in a pocked sandpaper finish. Also happens when the spray gun is held too far from the surface.

Filigree – The fine decorative accents around the main elements of the design.

Firing the Edge – Giving the edge of the line a splintered look.

Flathead – 1932-53 Ford or Mercury V-8 valve-in-block engine.

Getting a Set – Allowing a painted design enough time to dry.

Gloved Up – Wearing gloves.

Gold Sizing – A type of paint used for varnishing gold leaf surfaces.

Gilding – Applying gold leaf to a surface.

Gun Sighting – Looking down the line from one end (such as, in a barrel of a gun) to ensure that it is straight - i.e., "on target."

Hairline – A very fine line, finer than 1/64th (0.39688 mm) of an inch in width.

Hemi – Engine equipped with hemispherical combustion chambers in the heads, produced by Chrysler between 1951-57 and 1964-71.

Holiday – An area missing or with poor paint coverage.

Indexing Marks – The marks outlining the limits of a design or pattern (used mostly when marking door edges and bodylines).

Inline – A line painted inside another line (or letter).

Lead Sled – A custom car, derived from the fact that lead was used for reshaping bodies.

Lifting – In certain conditions, and as it dries, the chemicals in paint reacting to surface or atmospheric conditions causing a wrinkling, or "lift" of the painted surface.

Load – The paint carried by the brush after dipping.

Loose and Patent Gold Leaf – Books of gold leaf are available as loose sheets of leaf between paper (for use indoors), or loosely stuck to a paper backing (Patent Leaf), for use in breezy conditions – e.g., at motor shows.

Loosening up the paint – Thinning paint, so a better "flow" is achieved when applying with a brush.

Lowrider – A type of car that rides extremely low; often has elaborate paint jobs, upholstery, and decorative details inside and out.

Mashing it Down – Applying pressure.

Morgue File – A scrapbook of creative inspiration: magazine and newspaper cuttings, photos of designs, found objects, and pressings from nature.

Outline – A line outside a wider line (or letter).

Paint System – Proprietory paint process with respect to paints, primers, mixers, and recommended drying times.

Palletting – Loading a brush with paint.

Panel Art – Pinstriping applied to a panel intended for wall display.

Panel Jam – A gathering of pinstripers to paint panels on site, discuss pinstriping and sign art, and have a few drinks in the process.

Pouncing – When using paper patterns (usually for spraying), employing a spiked wheel to create perforations in the paper.

Pounce Bag – A rag filled with chalk, baby powder or lamp black.

Pock Marks – Moon-crater-shaped holes on the paint surface caused by exposure to silicone contamination.

Quarter Line – A finely outlined line, 1/4 inch in width.

Shop Towel – A cleaning-up rag.

Tape Burn – When tape is applied to a painted surface which hasn't dried, leaving an imprint, or "burn."

Tap Test – Tapping or very lightly stroking the surface with the fingers to see how dry it is.

Tick Mark – A short stroke or dot made on the surface with a pencil or Stabillo to show a point of measurement.

Wet on Wet – Spraying over a wet base coat paint, resulting in a glossy finish during blending.

Wrinkling – the wrinkling of a paint surface, usually caused by a chemical reaction of two incompatible solvents.

SELECTED BIBLIOGRAPHY

Advanced Pinstripe Art: How-To Secrets from the Masters
Timothy Remus
Wolfgang Productions, 2005
ISBN: 1929133324

Barris Kustom Techniques of the 50s Volume 4: Flames, Scallops, Paneling and Striping
George Barris
Motorbooks International, 1998
ISBN: 0965200531

Cool Cars, High Art: The Rise of Kustom Kulture
John Dewitt
University Press of Mississippi, 2002
ISBN: 1578064031

Customized: Art Inspired by Hot Rods, Low Riders, and American Car Culture
C. Brenda Jo, Chavoya Bright
Harry N Abrams, 2000
ISBN: 0810957272

Custom Lettering and Pinstriping Techniques: Vans, Rods, Bikes
S. T. Golson
Eastwood Co, 1995
ISBN: 0964147025

Dean Jeffries's Vintage Pinstriping
Dean Jeffries
Thaxton Press, 2001
ISBN: 0965200590

Driving Me Wild: Nitro-Powered Outlaw Culture!
Leah M. Kerr
PowerHouse Books, 2000
ISBN: 096510429X

Ed "Big Daddy" Roth: His Life, Times, Cars, and Art
Pat Ganahl
CarTech, 2003
ISBN: 1884089682

Kenneth Howard / Von Dutch
St John Morton
St. John Design Studio, 2001
ISBN: 0970088132

Mild to Wild Pinstriping
Tramp Warner
St Books, 1997
ISBN: 0918399157

Pinstriping
Ed Roth
Ed "Big Daddy" Roth, 1981
ASIN: B00070UGDO

Kustom Art Style
Neko Publishing Co. LTD., 2004
ISBN:777001253

Kustom Kulture: Ed "Big Daddy" Roth, Robert Williams and Others
Ron Turner
Last Gasp, 1993
ISBN: 0867194057

Pinstriping and Vehicle Graphics
John Hanukaine
Signcraft, 1997
ISBN: 0918399092

Rat Fink: The Art of Ed "Big Daddy" Roth
Douglas Nason, Greg Escalante
Last Gasp, 2003
ISBN: 0867195444

The Art of Freehand Pinstriping
Dick Bird
Eastwood Co, 1994
ISBN: 0964147009

The Art of Von Dutch
Aaron Kahan, Douglas Nason, Al Quattrocchi, Jeff Smith
Tornado Design LLC, 2006
ISBN: 0977111814

Truck Lettering, Pinstriping & Graphics
Gary D. Steele
ST Publications, 1994
ISBN: 0944094023

Von Dutch: The Art, the Myth, the Legend
Pat Ganahl
Brooklands Books, 2005
ISBN: 1884089984

13
SHOEI
Colonel Greengrass
SPEED & CUSTOM
GENUINE PARTS Service
VFO 686
2WCT919
Rock 'n' Roll
FORD
Holley
SYSTEM 1
MOON RACING CAMS
BUGPACK
BOSCH

2WCT919
Cabriolet
the Ultimate in
Pinstriping
by MAYNERD
and
WIERDO SHIRTS
Welcome to our Wedding Reception
GMC
ROCK, RODS & RAT FINKS!
DXT 446
Kawasaki
MAYUMI
Jan. 25. '14
PONTIAC
CVG 146F

MAZE
·06·